Logically Jesus

A Simple Presentation of Evidence
That Builds a Case for Christianity

Jerry Griffin

WESTBOW
P R E S S®
A DIVISION OF THOMAS NELSON
& ZONDERVAN

WestBow Press books may be ordered through booksellers or by contacting:

WestBow Press
A Division of Thomas Nelson & Zondervan
1663 Liberty Drive
Bloomington, IN 47403
www.westbowpress.com
844-714-3454

Because of the dynamic nature of the Internet, any web addresses or
links contained in this book may have changed since publication and
may no longer be valid. The views expressed in this work are solely those
of the author and do not necessarily reflect the views of the publisher,
and the publisher hereby disclaims any responsibility for them.

Any people depicted in stock imagery provided by Getty Images are
models, and such images are being used for illustrative purposes only.
Certain stock imagery © Getty Images.

ISBN: 978-1-9736-8871-6 (sc)
ISBN: 978-1-9736-8873-0 (hc)
ISBN: 978-1-9736-8872-3 (e)

Library of Congress Control Number: 2020905165

Print information available on the last page.

WestBow Press rev. date: 05/09/2022

Contents

Acknowledgments

First, I want to thank Amy, my daughter, for being the Christian example and inspiration I needed to delve into Christianity. She also provided valuable input to the writing of this book with various ideas and helping me determine its structure and format.

Second, even though they have gone on to be with the Lord, I want to thank my mother and father, who provided such great love and guidance to me as I grew up. The values they instilled in me are what I always fall back on as I navigate my way through life.

Third, I want to thank my longtime Sunday school and Bible study teacher, Mr. Phil Crone, for being such a great Bible teacher and providing background information about the Bible, especially the Hebrew customs and traditions that I would probably never have gotten from anyone else. Many times in this book, I rely on biblical information obtained from him over the years.

Finally, I want to thank the authors of the books and articles that I reference in this book. I give them all the credit for their expertise, which added tremendously to my work here.

Introduction

Logically Jesus was not initially conceived as a book. Instead, it was developed through an incremental process, as described below, over several years. For those of you contemplating how on earth anyone can possibly believe there is a god—an eternal creator—and that the Bible is indeed accurate, perhaps my journey will provide some enlightenment and create a desire in your heart to discover the truth for yourself.

This book should not be misconstrued as being about me. It is about a search for God and Christianity in which I am used only as a vessel to portray that pursuit.

I was brought up in a home with great Christian parents. My family attended church every week, and thus I considered myself to be a Christian believer. After I attended college and left home to live on my own, I no longer relied on my parents to provide the Christian guidance I so badly needed. My interests were directed more to other things, and I rarely attended church. Consequently I drifted from my Christian upbringing, became a skeptic through indoctrination and began to question the truth of the Bible and Christianity—I drank the Kool-Aid. I still wanted the Bible and Christianity to be true, but I wasn't totally sure anymore. I had many questions such as:

- Was the earth created as described in the book of Genesis?
- Are we the result of evolution as proposed by Charles Darwin, or was there a creator of all things?

- Were the people and events portrayed in the Bible real?
- Was Jesus a real person?
- Was Jesus the Son of God who died for our sins on the cross and was resurrected, or was He just a good person and teacher, as some believe?
- Is there a real heaven and a real hell and do angels and demons exist?
- Are there real evidences that support the truth of the Bible and Christianity?

Still young, I figured that if the Bible and Christianity were indeed true, I had plenty of time to figure it all out anyway. However, after many years my reasoning changed and chapter 3 describes the process I went through in sorting all this out to become a true Christian.

Over time I began talking to people who were skeptics, like I had been before I found Christianity, and considering how I could help them come to that same realization of the truth. My initial intention was to write a few things that I could share with others, but as time went by, I thought of more things to add. I decided to separate the information into topics, which eventually led me to consider creating a book, and that is how *Logically Jesus* was developed.

The book presents evidence that supports the truth and accuracy of the Bible, as well as the importance of knowing where we stand concerning our religious beliefs. It is intentionally written on a simple level using what I consider common-sense arguments and examples, so that anyone can understand the concepts being conveyed. The intended audience is the average person, who has not studied science or the Bible in depth. People highly educated in those areas have access to many detailed intellectual books that support a belief in Christianity. The book was written primarily for skeptics of Christianity, but also to Christians to a lesser degree. I hope that some Christians can find inspiration from certain topics and maybe some things they might use in their defense of Christianity to others. Below is an overall summary of the contents of *Logically Jesus*:

✓ Arguments are made to support the belief that the universe did not always exist but required an eternal creator for its existence.

✓ An attempt is made to provide support that, given the matter of the universe, living things did not just evolve through random chance mutations and natural selection, but instead required a supernatural creator and designer.

✓ Common themes propagated throughout the Bible, the harmonies of the four Gospels, how the Jewish feasts point to Jesus as the Messiah, and health instructions given to the Israelites in the Old Testament centuries before germs were known to man are discussed.

✓ Certain biblical events and personal experiences that cannot be explained as coincidences are discussed.

✓ The accuracy of the Bible is supported by archeological finds that verify the existence of people, places, and events portrayed in the Bible. I describe the fulfillment of several Old Testament prophecies concerning these discoveries.

✓ References are made to historical documents that lend support to the Bible.

✓ Reasoning is given why Jesus had to have existed as a real person and as the Messiah, as described in the Bible, and how the disciples and early Christians lend credibility to the resurrection of Jesus on the third day after His crucifixion.

✓ Several Old Testament prophecies are discussed about a Messiah that were fulfilled by Jesus Christ down to the smallest detail.

✓ Several Old Testament and New Testament prophecies are discussed that provide evidence for the Bible and Christianity, and how we are fast approaching the last days before Jesus Christ will return.

The first three chapters give background for why I wrote the book, my perspective on Christianity, and my personal testimony. Chapters 4 through 6 focus on scientific explanations, although they are kept simple so that one does not have to be a rocket scientist to comprehend the concepts presented. Chapters 8 through 18 lean more heavily on Bible scriptures, archeology, and documents that support the Bible.

Chapter 19 attempts to mathematically show how the evidence presented throughout the book overwhelmingly suggests the Bible is indeed accurate and was written under the divine guidance of God. Chapters 20 and 21 provide final thoughts and conclusions about salvation and eternity.

The numbered references are organized by chapter in the last section of this book titled *Notes*. URLs for internet articles referenced were valid at the dates included in the reference list. Permission was obtained for all references cited in the *Notes* that were not in the public domain. Things presented as facts not cited were from the author's personal knowledge accumulated over the years from formal schooling, teaching experience, individual research, and Bible study. All Bible quotations are taken from the King James Version.

If you're looking for proof that the Bible is God's inspired Word, you won't find it here. I don't pretend to give proof, because I think it is impossible to provide. However, I do think you will find things that support a belief in Christianity. You must be willing to open your mind and heart and hear about Christianity. All I can do is share a few of my ideas, and then it's up to you to choose which road to take.

Part One

Laying the Foundation

One

A Bit of Groundwork

I realize there are Christians, including many pastors, who think a book that attempts to provide evidence for Christianity is unnecessary, since the Bible is all that is needed. They proclaim that no one should question Christianity, but instead that we should just accept it and believe in God and the Bible. I agree that the Bible is sufficient for people who have a good knowledge of its contents and maintain a personal relationship with Jesus Christ.

However, many people never read the Bible or go to church. They have not been exposed to Christianity to any significant extent and thus have little basis for belief in it. As a result, they tend to reject the notion of Christianity being true. I know that God can make anyone a believer anytime He wants, but the simple fact is that there are many skeptics, agnostics, and atheists in our world.

Some people look down on Christians as being misinformed. Many people have been indoctrinated by schools where Bible reading, prayer, and the study of creationism have been banned in favor of evolution, which is taught as fact rather than theory. Many people think the Bible is just a collection of fairy tales; they have never read the Bible and know nothing about it except through hearsay or atheistic indoctrination.

Miracles are events with no known scientific explanation,

which makes it hard for some people to believe in them. The Bible documents many miracles performed by God; His Son, Jesus; and others. Maybe this is a point of contention among skeptics, agnostics, or atheists who have a difficult time believing that these miracles could actually have happened. However, miracles are certainly possible, because events that we call miracles happen every day, often through divine intervention.

Some people are turned off by Christianity because they see certain self-proclaimed Christians as hypocrites. I have heard people say that although certain Christians are in church anytime the doors are open, those same Christians are seen to exhibit undesirable behavior when they are not in church. As a result, such Christians are seen as going to church for social purposes and to further their business relationships in the community rather than to worship God.

These non-Christians are often good people. In my experience, many are more honest, live better lives, and are more willing to help others than some professed Christians. It's a shame that a few Christian hypocrites can have such a negative effect on others.

Some people don't want to believe in Christianity no matter what, or they just don't care. That baffles me, because if Christianity is true, wouldn't they want to know? If Christianity is true and they are not Christian, they will regret it for eternity. How could anyone afford to take that risk?

There are many diverse opinions and beliefs about the universe and spiritual world. Some believe there is no god and that the universe was not created but has always existed. To them, this life is all there is; there is nothing more beyond it, and religion is just a waste of time. Some people believe in religions other than Christianity and are willing to give their lives to promote those religions. Some believe that various gods control certain aspects of our world. Some believe in the God of the Old Testament but dispute the fact that Jesus is the Son of God, whereas others believe in the teachings of Christianity. Then there are people who don't know what to believe.

Unbelief in God doesn't imply a general lack of knowledge. Some of the most brilliant scientists of all time didn't believe in God until their own scientific and/or mathematical research gave them overwhelming evidence for the necessity of a creator. A number of skeptics have become Christians and even ministers after seeing evidence that supports the Bible.

The objective of this book is to provide a small sample of evidence for Christianity from several disciplines. You may disagree with what I determine as evidence for certain topics, but I believe that if you look at all the topics, you'll agree that evidence does truly exist for Christianity. I firmly believe that if anyone seeks God, He is more than willing to reveal Himself to them.

Apologetics is a discipline that attempts to bring people to Christianity by presenting various kinds of evidence—in such fields as astronomy, archeology, and microbiology, as well as the Bible and non-biblical texts—for the God of the Bible. Many books and articles supporting this effort are available, and the authors tend to make detailed, in-depth arguments in the discussion of their specific topic. In contrast, my intent is to provide more general information from a broad perspective from several areas that is very basic and simple to understand. It is my hope that at least some of these topics will provoke thought by the reader.

In my study of science I have filtered things that I've read, thought about them deeply, and come to my own conclusions. I am much more willing to believe in something that seems logical, rather than in something totally theoretical. I realize, however, there are people who have opposing viewpoints.

At one time, I had only limited knowledge of the Bible even though I had attended church most of my life. My Sunday school classes were good, but they mostly involved moral lessons about life using a few selected scriptures rather than delving into the scriptures in much depth. As I discuss in chapter 3, I decided that I really needed to study the scriptures in greater detail to determine whether they were written under the divine guidance of God.

If you have little knowledge of the Bible and Christianity, how can you evaluate its validity? You have no frame of reference for any argument for or against it. Perhaps a little study into Christianity might start you thinking. That is my hope. I think a person should be certain about what they believe and able to defend their position. Is the existence of religions other than Christianity supported by evidence? It is easy to declare belief in various religious doctrines and beliefs, but can that belief be verified in some way? Ideally, you will see that there is real evidence for Christianity.

Two

Determine Our Religious Belief/Unbelief

In Matthew 7:13–14, Jesus says, "Enter ye in at the strait gate: for wide is the gate, and broad is the way, that leadeth to destruction, and many there be which go in thereat: Because strait is the gate, and narrow is the way, which leadeth unto life, and few there be that find it." Based upon the state of our society today, which I believe is in an irreversible continual downward spiral, I think Jesus was spot-on. Which gate will you enter when your life is over on earth? Will you be like many and go the way that leads to destruction, or will you be of the few who enter the gate that leads to eternal life with God?

Suppose you knew that you were going to die tomorrow afternoon at three o'clock. How would you spend the last few hours of your life? What would be your thoughts about the hereafter? If you are a skeptic, would you make it a priority to somehow determine if Christianity is true and whether you could become a Christian as your departure from this life approaches? Or would you be concerned only with saying your goodbyes to your family and friends, whom you believe you will never see again, and finalizing your funeral arrangements? Well, someday your time will come. It will come for all of us, for no one is exempt.

Either the teachings of Christianity are true or they are not. If they are true and you are not a believer, then you will regret it for all eternity. Nothing you have accomplished or accumulated on earth will matter. If these teachings are not true, your only regret may be the little time you invested in studying the possibilities.

Many people reject Christianity because they think it would restrict their lives and prevent them from pursuing their earthly desires. They see being a Christian as an obstacle that would get in the way of having fun. They cannot imagine being a Christian and still living the life they want. Such people don't realize that being a Christian would make their lives fuller, more enjoyable, and with less worry about what tomorrow may bring.

Many people just go about their daily lives thinking that what's important are material things—money, nice homes, expensive cars, great jobs, and so on—and there's nothing wrong with wanting and having those things. But the more material things people have, the more they want, so that they're never really satisfied. Once we die, those material things are no longer important anyway because we can't take them with us. As the old saying goes, "You never see a U-Haul trailer behind a hearse."

Being from Alabama, and as a sports enthusiast, I'm familiar with the Auburn/Alabama football rivalry. To many people in this state, this game is an annual life-or-death situation. Some people think it's more important than anything else in life, including religion, politics, and even family. Many football fans can tell you the names of all the players and their positions on the team they support, but they can't name the four Gospels of the Bible. I just wonder how important that game will be when their time has come to meet their maker.

People who put such high priority on earthly things must not really comprehend the ramifications of the destiny of their souls after they die. When people face death, they won't be worried about how much real estate they own, how much money they have stashed away, or how popular they are. The score of a football game won't mean a hill of beans. At that time, the only thing of importance will be where they spend eternity. Nothing else will matter.

When nonbelievers are on their deathbed, the possibility of eternity becomes real and urgent to many of them. Many people acknowledge God and accept Jesus Christ as their Lord and Savior just before death. When they are in distress, it is always God they seem to turn to. Many have been known to cry out, "God, please have mercy on me." It's amazing what effect imminent death has on people as they approach that final moment of their life.

Many of us tend to ignore God if everything—health, relationships, finances, and so on—is going well for us. But as soon as something goes terribly wrong, we call on God and expect His help immediately. We blame Him if He doesn't respond in a positive way for us. In doing this, are we really being fair to God? Although God is merciful and loves us, why should we expect His help when we have ignored Him?

Every one of us needs to determine whether we can believe in Christianity while we still have that chance. We never know when the breath we take will be our last. The choice we make will determine our eternal destiny. Eternity is a long time—forever. Our life on earth is less than the time it takes to snap your fingers as compared with eternity. Even if you live to old age, when compared with eternity, your life will have been so short that mathematically it could be considered as zero.

I heard a sermon titled "Keep Eternity in Mind" on the radio by Dr. Erwin Lutzer, pastor of Moody Church in Chicago, in which he gave an analogy of just how long eternity is. Here's my paraphrase of his analogy:

> Suppose a bird from another solar system flew to earth once every thousand years and each time picked up a grain of sand with its beak and took it back to the other system. When all the earth had been carried away, eternity would only have begun.[1]

Some say that science is proving the Bible to be wrong. But as a result of their scientific research and discoveries, more and more scientists are becoming believers in God. It seems reasonable that if these brilliant minds believe in God, then maybe those of us with only average intelligence should at least take notice.

How could anyone ignore the possibility of our God and the promises offered in His Bible? Jesus promises to His believers a wonderful eternal life with Him, but to unbelievers a life of eternal damnation apart from God. God says clearly in His Bible that He is going to have His day of reckoning (judgment), and I am sure He will. We'd best be ready for that occasion.

Most of us have lost family members and good friends who were Christians. If they were right in their Christian beliefs, don't you want to be with them when you depart from this earth? I know that I want to spend eternity with my Christian family and friends who have gone on to be with the Lord.

Just think how great it will be to see them again in the presence of our Lord forever in a place that is indescribably beautiful. In that place, there are no bad people or sin, no one lacks for anything, we never get sick, and we live forever. On a lighthearted note, I hope for lots of chocolate and nice golf courses. Or are you content to not worry about it and take your chances? An eternal life with Jesus doesn't cost anything—it's free. All that is required is that you believe in the Lord Jesus Christ and accept Him as your Lord and Savior.

Three

From Skeptic to Christian

Some people reject Christianity and will have nothing to do with it. Their minds are already made up, and they are so opposed to Christianity that they won't give it an inkling of consideration. Many have a paradigm of atheism and will try to make any evidence of any kind support that ideology no matter what. Christianity doesn't seem to be even a remote possibility for them. The only way these people will be converted is by the divine intervention of God on their behalf. In some cases, this has happened, such as with the apostle Paul as documented in Acts 9.

At the other end of the spectrum are people who are exposed to Christianity at an early age and never consider anything else as the truth. The unquestionable knowledge of God's truth and salvation plan is instilled in them. Like a child's willingness to trust their parents, they accept the teachings of Christianity.

Somewhere in between are people who are exposed to Christianity and want to believe, but still question its validity. Many of these skeptics require evidence of Christianity's truth. I once fell into this category, and my quest for evidence led me to extensive research, study, and thought. The answers I found convinced me that the Bible is the accurate Word of God and Christianity is the true religion. My road to Jesus has been a long journey with many hills, valleys, and obstacles along the way.

My parents were strong Christians, and they did their best to teach their faith to their children and serve as Christian examples for others. My father was a respected and godly man, a schoolteacher and principal by profession, and I never heard a negative comment about him from anyone. That is amazing, considering the thousands of students, parents, teachers, and others with whom he dealt for more than forty years.

My dad performed the duties of principal, ninth-grade teacher, secretary, janitor, maintenance person, and basketball and baseball coach. He also supervised all other school events and activities involved with his principalship at a small rural school in southern Alabama. Also, he was the lone adult Sunday school teacher at the small rural church we attended.

After my older brothers left home, I helped my dad with his many duties. He needed help, and I was the only one available, so we were always together during my nine years at his school. As a result, we were close, and I learned firsthand about his professionalism, morals, values, integrity, honesty, hard work, love for others, and Christian faith. My dad took his faith and responsibilities very seriously. They say behind every good man is a good woman, and my mother certainly fits that description. My mother was a housewife that always supported my dad in everything, and everyone that knew her loved her just like they did my dad.

Even though I had much exposure to Christianity starting at an early age, I was lackadaisical concerning my attention to salvation for many years of my life. I was more interested in other things, like having a good time and establishing a good working career. I regret that I didn't become a true Christian earlier so that I could have been a much better example to others over the years.

I attended college and majored in mathematics with physical science and biological science minors. My career consisted of being a mathematician for the Department of the Army and teaching both mathematics and science at the high school level and mathematics at the college level. Mathematics instilled in me the need to think logically (hence the title of this book, *Logically Jesus*), and the sciences instilled in me the need to seek reasons for why and how things happen.

In the many science courses I took, from elementary school through college, that dealt with the origin of the species, Darwin's theory of evolution was taught as the gospel. (No pun intended.) Science textbooks would illustrate with a sequence of drawings the various stages in the development of man, beginning with an ape-like creature and ending with modern man. Even though it didn't concern me too much at the time, I realized there was a fundamental conflict between the theory of evolution and the Bible's account of creation. I was especially concerned that the origin of the first ape-like creature was never addressed.

The birth of my daughter had a profound influence on my life. She was a devout Christian from the time she was old enough to comprehend God and His plan of salvation through His Son Jesus Christ. Her steadfast faith in Christianity made a great impression on me which caused me to begin some serious soul-searching about Christianity and eternity. That led me to extensive research in which I searched for any evidence that I could find to support the truth of Christianity. I researched topics in apologetics and read all kinds of articles, both religious and scientific.

I was divorced, and my little daughter would visit me on the weekends. She always insisted that we go to church, where I started to pay more attention to the sermons and Sunday school lessons. I started attending a Bible study class, and the more I studied and researched, the more God revealed the truth of Christianity to me. I believe that as I began to seek God, He was more than willing to reach out to me. Matthew 7:7 says, "Ask, and it shall be given you; seek, and ye shall find; knock, and it shall be opened unto you."

After some time, I had obtained abundant evidence that convinced me of the truth of Christianity, although I became a Christian just as much from seeking God and Him reciprocating. For the first time, I knew in my heart that Christianity was the true religion. I no longer needed evidence; in fact, God just used my desire for evidence as a mechanism to reach me.

Not too long after that, I went with a group of people on a tour of the Holy Land in Israel. This trip provided much inspiration and biblical verification to me as we walked where Jesus and His disciples had walked.

Over the last few years, I have had discussions with people who were in about the same place in their spiritual life that I was before I truly found Christianity. I wrote this book to share my thoughts and maybe some helpful information with people who are looking for evidence supporting the Bible. However, I can present only a small sample of the many evidences I found in a short book like this, and I try to use a simple common-sense approach that doesn't require the reader to have a science or theology degree. I write this with a humble heart and certainly don't pretend to be someone that I am not. I don't teach Sunday school or even a Bible study class—just someone who wants to share some thoughts with those who are Christian skeptics.

Although I profess to be a Christian, I don't claim to be better than anyone else. I have certainly made my share of mistakes (nothing illegal) and continue to make them every day. Christians are not perfect; we are all sinners who need the grace of God. We are all God's creation, and He loves us regardless of our thoughts or actions—what we have or haven't done. My spiritual development has been a gradual process over the years toward a closer relationship with Jesus Christ, and I consider myself a continual work in progress by the Lord. Due to my imperfections and shortcomings, I sometimes questioned my worthiness to write a book on Christianity. But I truly believe the Lord was guiding me in this effort to promote Christianity, even if to a small degree.

I still have questions about things such as our universe, our existence, and the spiritual world, and I realize that only God can answer those questions. However, I know now that the Bible is the true and accurate Word of God, and my wish is for others to know this too.

Part Two

Evidence for a Personal Eternal Creator

Four

A Creator Is Required

We need to look at more than just pure science in our quest for a creator. It is my contention that if people really look at the total picture while keeping an open mind, most will acknowledge that a creator is required. The evidence from several areas throughout this book will provide much support for my belief in a creator. Let's first look at some science.

Which seems more likely? (a) Lifeless matter, which either has always existed or appeared out of nothing, and miraculously produced complex living organisms, including man, through random mutations and natural selection; or (b) a creator was involved in the design and development of all the marvelous complex living organisms we have today. One or the other must be true, and that is the basic question we will be dealing with in this chapter and the next three.

As stated earlier, many detailed books have been written on the subject of creation versus evolution that go into great depth, but this is not one of them. My discussion of science is deliberately simple, and I shall try to keep this book very basic and understandable to most anyone.

Nothing but Nothing from Nothing

No scientist has ever shown how something came to be all on its own. In "Nothing Left to Chance," part of a teaching series by R. C. Sproul, we find these words:

> Nothing can create itself. Nothing can do nothing. ... Ladies and gentlemen, if anything exists now—this is elementary—then there never could have been a time when there was nothing. Because the most fundamental maxim of all reason, and all science, and all philosophy is the maxim, *'ex nihilo nihil fit'* out of nothing, nothing comes.[1]

Sproul's statement makes complete, logical sense to me. Since our universe exists, there never was a time when there was absolutely nothing. The universe didn't appear on its own out of nothing. Therefore either the universe has always existed or an eternal supernatural being created it.

Famous Scientists

Some of our most famous and respected scientists of all time support the notion of a supernatural creator. Their belief in God may be the greatest evidence in support of a creator. There are scientists who deny the existence of a creator, but more and more are becoming believers. In "25 Famous Scientists on God," Javier Ordovas quotes twenty-five famous scientists concerning their belief in a creator. Here is one of those quotes:

> Isaac Newton (1643–1727), founder of classical theoretical physics: "The admirable arrangement and harmony of the universe could only have come from the plan of an omniscient and omnipotent Being."[2]

Other quotes by famous scientists in the aforementioned internet article by Javier Ordovas also suggest a creator. If I were still a skeptic, I would have to take a hard look into the possibility of God based on the beliefs of these twenty-five scientists, universally recognized as some of the most brilliant minds of all time with intelligence far superior to most people. Why would one be inclined to dismiss their beliefs?

There are several theories about the age of our universe. In the following section, I address observations by experts about these theories, along with a few thoughts concerning the requirement for a creator.

Three Theories of Our Universe

I. The Universe Has Always Existed and Was Not Created

We rightly assume that complex, highly structured things in our material world have been designed and assembled by someone. We know that computers, cars, airplanes, skyscrapers, nuclear reactors, and so on, because of their complexity, were designed and created by someone. These things are simple when you compare them with a human being. It seems logical that since we know the simpler things had to be designed, then we should believe something much more complex and perfect, such as the human body, also had to be designed and created.

Structure of Atoms and Molecules

Let's now consider the most basic structure in our universe, the atom, which makes up all matter. Atoms are highly structured from various particles—electrons, protons, neutrons, and others. Protons and neutrons make up the atom's nucleus, with electrons revolving around the nucleus at definite orbital levels, much like planets revolving around the sun. What distinguishes one kind of atom from another is the different numbers of these various particles. All the atoms of a specific element—such as hydrogen, oxygen, sodium, or silver—are identical, and there are more than a hundred known elements.

Atoms bond together through a complex process of sharing valence electrons in their outer shells to form molecules, which constitute substances (compounds). For example, two hydrogen atoms join with one oxygen atom to create an H_2O molecule, recognized as water. Similarly two hydrogen atoms and two oxygen atoms join to create an H_2O_2 molecule, which is hydrogen peroxide. The various combinations and numbers of different atoms are what make the different compounds that have such different properties.

If we are to believe that the universe, and thus matter, has always existed, then we must ask how all these different kinds of basic atoms with their structured components were in place for all eternity *without a cause.* We must ask how the mechanisms came about that facilitated the bonding of these complex atoms to form the various inorganic molecules that supposedly later interacted to form organic molecules of which life is made *without a cause.* To believe that matter, with its complex structure, has existed for all eternity is blind faith. It is my contention that a higher being was instrumental in putting the basic structure of matter into place.

DNA, RNA, and Proteins

Dr. Hugh Ross is an astronomer, astrophysicist, author, and founder of the Christian organization Reasons to Believe. In his book *The Creator and the Cosmos,* Ross says this:

> Molecules responsible for life chemistry cannot function by themselves. DNA (molecules that hold the blueprints for the construction of life molecules), proteins (molecules that follow portions of the blueprints in building and repairing life molecules), and RNA (molecules that carry the blueprints from the DNA to specific proteins) are all interdependent. Thus, for life to originate mechanistically, all

three kinds of molecules would need to emerge
spontaneously and simultaneously from inorganic
compounds.[3]

Regarding the simultaneous appearance of DNA, RNA, and
proteins, Ross makes the following observation:

> Even the most optimistic of researchers agreed that
> the chance appearance of these incredibly complex
> molecules at exactly the same time and place was
> beyond the realm of natural possibility.[4]

DNA, RNA, and protein molecules had to have been created at
the same time and place, so they could function together. Any one
is useless without the others. Without question, the requirement for
the simultaneous appearance of these complex molecules certainly
provides great evidence for a creator.

The Cell

The cell is the basic unit of life. All the features of a living cell must
be operational for it to live and function properly. A single living cell,
either plant or animal, consists of many individual components, with
each performing its specialized function and working in conjunction
with all the other components. That is true for even the simplest of
living cells, such as a bacterium. If any component is not operational,
the cell is severely degraded and usually cannot live.

I must then ask the question: How did the first living cell come
into existence? How did all these required cellular components come
about at the same time, put into place and able to interact to produce
a functioning living cell? Without question, a creator is required
not only to construct each of the components, but also to put them
together to make the first living, functioning cell.

Second Law of Thermodynamics

The laws of thermodynamics are accepted as valid throughout the scientific world. The second law of thermodynamics says that entropy will usually increase over time in an isolated system that has not yet reached equilibrium. Entropy is the lack of order in a system over time, resulting in disorder or chaos. Entropy goes against the concept of evolution, because evolution requires that organisms become more organized or developed to better enhance their chance of survival in their environment.

Our universe, as we know it, is an isolated system. We have no evidence that there are other universes to share energy or matter with our own. We can therefore conclude that it tends toward entropy.

Dr. Danny R. Faulkner, in "Does the Second Law of Thermodynamics Favor Evolution?" says,

> "Technically, the second law of thermodynamics applies to the universe as a whole. The entropy of the universe cannot decrease, though it may increase, and it often does. Thus, the universe has an ever-increasing entropy burden. If the universe were eternal, the universe would have had more than ample time to have reached a state of maximum entropy. We observe that the universe is far from a state of maximum entropy, so the universe cannot be eternal."[5]

In "Second Law of Thermodynamics," from the All About Science website, we read,

> "The implications of the Second Law of Thermodynamics are considerable. The universe is constantly losing usable energy and never gaining. We logically conclude the universe is not eternal. The universe had a finite beginning—the moment at which it was at 'zero entropy' (its most ordered

possible state). Like a wind-up clock, the universe is winding down, as if at one point it was fully wound up and has been winding down ever since. The question is who wound up the clock?"[6]

I have an answer to the question "Who wound up the clock?" It was a supernatural creator of the universe, who is our God.

II. Long Creation Period

Many scientists believe that the universe was formed billions of years ago through what scientists call the big bang. How did that happen? Was the big bang a gigantic explosion out of nothing, caused by no one, in which all the matter of the universe was created? It seems impossible that a big bang event could yield matter from nothing.

People who hold to a long creation believe that God created the universe, but not in six days of twenty-four hours each; instead, they interpret the book of Genesis as advocating for time intervals longer than days. There are varying beliefs about how God did this. In *The Fingerprint of God,* Hugh Ross supports the big bang theory but explains it as follows:

> Expansion, coupled with deceleration, indicates a universe that is exploding outward from a point. In fact, through the equations of general relativity, we can trace that "explosion" backward to its origin, an instant when the entire physical universe burst forth from a single point of infinite density. That instant when the universe originated from a point of no size at all is called the singularity. ... The singularity is not really a point. It is the whole of three dimensional space compressed to zero size.[7]

In an explosion, the fragments would travel outward fast at the beginning but decelerate over time. According to Ross, this motion is what is happening with the galaxies in our universe, thus the term *big bang explosion.* The single point of infinite density that Dr. Ross refers to is something—not nothing. So the big bang theory really starts with something. It didn't occur out of nothing. I must ask the question: What was the origin of the single point of infinite density?

Ross says in Table 9.3, labeled "The age of the universe from direct observations," that using three measuring methods, the universe's "mean age = 16.3 ± 3 billion years."[8] This sixteen, plus or minus three, billion years is a finite (definite) time interval. Estimates by other scientists who believe in a long creation vary, but they are all no more than billions of years. Regardless of the time interval, anything that has existed for only a finite time must have been created and thus required a creator for its existence. It didn't appear all on its own.

Some believe God used the big bang to create the universe from an infinitesimal mass of infinite density and allowed evolution to take place over an extremely long period of time to form the complex living organisms, including man, that we have today from inorganic matter. Some believe He created simple living matter that evolved into complex species that we have today over an extremely long period of time. Others believe that God created all living species without the benefit of evolution, but that He did it over a long period.

III. *Short Creation Period*

Still another theory suggests that the universe came into existence during a short creation period and that earth is only a few thousand years old. A creator could certainly have placed the universe in its current configuration of observed expansion and deceleration that astronomers and scientists have described without the necessity of the big bang event. This belief allows the possibility that the universe has existed for a much shorter time.

There is much archeological evidence for a young earth. The article "Six Evidences of a Young Earth," by *Answers in Genesis,* offers several such evidences, of which I find the following to be the most intriguing and compelling:

> When solid rock is bent, it normally cracks and breaks. Rock can only bend without fracturing when it is softened by extreme heating (which causes re-crystallization) or when the sediments have not yet fully hardened. There are numerous locations around the world (including the famous Grand Canyon) where we observe massive sections of strata that have been tightly folded, without evidence of the sediments being heated. This is a major problem for evolutionists who believe these rock layers were laid down gradually over vast eons of time, forming the geologic record. However, it makes perfect sense to creationists who believe these layers were formed rapidly in the global, catastrophic Flood described in Genesis.[9]

You can find many more such articles on the internet that support the notion of a young earth, which requires a creator. I personally believe in a young earth that was created as described in the book of Genesis in which the time interval was six twenty-four-hour days rather than billions of years. I realize I cannot question God, but it seems more reasonable to me that He performed creation in days rather than over a span of billions of years. Nevertheless, it wouldn't bother me if I learned that God formed His creation over billions of years.

I also believe that since God created time, He had to be outside of time to create it, and thus is not bound by it. Regardless of how long it took, I believe He created all things, including all species of plants and animals, without evolution, as I discuss in the next two chapters.

The Heavens Declare the Glory of God

The universe is so large that it is difficult for us to comprehend its vastness. Light travels at approximately 186,000 miles per second, equivalent to more than seven times around the earth at the equator in only one second. When we look into the sky on a clear night, the light that reaches our eyes from a distant star may have left on its journey toward earth before Jesus was born.

The distance that light can travel at the rate of approximately 186,000 miles per second in a year is called a light-year—approximately 5,869,713,600,000 miles. Astronomers can see galaxies that are millions of light-years from the earth. Traveling at approximately 186,000 miles per second, it would take millions of years for light originating from those galaxies to reach the earth. Such mind-boggling numbers suggest that the creator of something as large as the universe would certainly have to be supernatural.

When King David wrote, "The heavens declare the glory of God; and the firmament sheweth his handiwork" (Psalm 19:1), he meant that the vastness of space, with all its heavenly bodies, shows the handiwork of God and is a testament to His glory. Even though King David didn't have the scientific knowledge we have today, he understood that only God could put something so vast and magnificent together.

I conclude with much conviction that the universe was not eternal. I believe that regardless of how long the process lasted, the universe was created, which required a supernatural creator. All of chapter 5, in which I reject evolution in favor of creation, as well as chapter 6, in which I present information that suggests that the world and all that is in it is complex and intricately designed to function together, could have been included in this chapter.

As far as I know, the only religions that deal with the subject of creation to much extent are those that support the teachings of the book of Genesis. I am more likely to believe in something that attempts to give a reasonable explanation than in something that offers little or no explanation at all.

Five

Scrapping the Theory of Evolution

Beliefs about evolution come in different varieties. Some people believe that organic matter originated from inorganic matter that has always existed, whereas others believe that God created the inorganic matter and allowed evolution to take place and create living things. There are others who believe that God created living organisms and that over long periods of time, these organisms developed into highly sophisticated organisms through evolution.

When I speak of evolution, I am referring to significant changes in a species over time that would lead to the development of a new species. Charles Darwin, considered to be the father of the theory of evolution, contends that species develop into other species by random chance mutations and natural selection. In "Natural Selection," chapter 4 of his famous book titled *On the Origin of Species*, Darwin writes this:

> Natural Selection acts, as we have seen, exclusively by
> the preservation and accumulation of variations, ...
> The ultimate result will be that each creature will
> tend to become more and more improved in relation
> to its conditions of life.[1]

When Darwin developed his theory and for many years afterward, relevant scientific fields such as biology, microbiology, botany, and archeology were not sufficiently advanced to develop a serious case against it, as I believe we have now. However, I do believe in microevolution, in which minor changes occur within a species over time.

In his theory of evolution, Darwin didn't commit to evolution of organic matter from inorganic matter, but he didn't refute the possibility either. In chapter 4 of *On the Origin of Species,* he writes this about his stance on the origin of evolution:

> looking to the dawn of life, when all organic beings, as we may imagine, presented the simplest structure, how could the first steps in advancement or in the differentiation and specialization of parts arise? I can make no sufficient answer, and can only say that we have no facts to guide us, and therefore that all speculations on this subject would be baseless and useless.[2]

Many people accept Darwin's theory of evolution as fact, even though, as its name says, it is *only a theory.* The burden of proof has always been on how we can disprove it. It's amazing how many people support evolution on blind faith alone. Most people with whom I have talked cannot give any concrete reasons why they believe in evolution—they just say that they believe it is possible.

Maybe they were educated in schools where Darwin's theory of evolution was taught as fact. For instance, many colleges employ predominantly faculty who promote evolution and refuse to teach the possibility of creationism. The rejection of creationism is also permeating into all levels of grade school. Or perhaps believers in evolution just agree with the arguments presented by scientists who are evolutionists, or maybe that's just what they *want* to believe.

If the evolutionists cannot provide irrefutable scientific evidence for evolution using the scientific method of investigation, they should say that the theory of evolution is only a theory and it should be presented as such in our schools. Creationism is another theory that should be taught as well, especially since many people in the United States favor creation over evolution as the mechanism in which complex living organisms came to be.

We should expect the proponents of evolution to provide many specific examples of how random chance mutations have resulted in fine gradations that allowed species to evolve and advance. All the many species of animals and plants should provide prolific evidence for evolution, if it does truly exist. If evolution is true, I believe it would be impossible to hide the evidence for it.

Some evolutionists believe that birds evolved from dinosaurs. If that's true, then we should expect them to describe the steps involved in that process. Sure, they have uncovered dinosaurs that have birdlike characteristics, but have they shown that one type of dinosaur developed into another through mutations? We have complete dinosaurs and birds in the archeological record, but if birds evolved from dinosaurs, there should be intermediate forms that illustrate the full lineage from dinosaur to bird. The early intermediate forms would exhibit mostly dinosaur characteristics, and the progression through evolution should exhibit more and more forms with birdlike characteristics, until finally an unmistakable bird species is the result.

Some evolutionists start with inorganic matter, commonly termed *prebiotic soup*, without attempting to explain its origin. The term *prebiotic* means "before life." These evolutionists visualize an ancient pond containing this prebiotic soup that contains all the inorganic chemicals necessary to create life. With the help of some unexplained source of energy, *wham!* Magically, organic compounds—amino acids which form proteins—supposedly appeared without any explanation. Even if all this were true, to me, the origin of the prebiotic pond and the source of energy is by far the most important question.

Even if one could assume the eternal presence of this slimy prebiotic soup from which all life has supposedly evolved, I question basic points about the concept of evolution as discussed in the following sections of this chapter.

Favorable vs. Harmful Mutations

Scientists agree that evolution from an organism to a slightly more advanced organism would have to result from mutations. Evolutionists base their whole theory on these mutations and survival of the fittest. Favorable mutations would help the species to survive better in its environment, whereas harmful mutations would have a negative effect. We learned in biology classes that certain inherited diseases—sickle cell anemia, cystic fibrosis, among many others—in humans are the result of gene mutations. Thus it appears to me that harmful mutations most likely occur more frequently than favorable mutations. If so, how would the total effect of mutations support evolution?

Evolution Requires Infinite Time

Many evolutionists believe that over an infinite period of time, organic matter can somehow evolve from inorganic matter. Based on Hugh Ross's assertion about the requirement for the simultaneous occurrence of DNA, RNA, and proteins, as discussed in the previous chapter, I contend that no matter how long inorganic matter has existed, organic matter could not have originated from it.

The Second Law of Thermodynamics

The second law of thermodynamics says that it applies to closed systems, such as our universe. But within the universe, the earth is considered an open system, and evolutionists therefore maintain that the law does not apply to evolution on earth. In "Does Entropy Contradict Evolution?" Dr. Henry M. Morris writes as follows:

> In the first place, the entropy principle applies at least as much to open systems as to closed systems.

In an isolated real system, shut off from external energy, the entropy (or disorganization) will always increase. In an open system (such as the earth receiving an influx of heat energy from the sun), the entropy always tends to increase, and, as a matter of fact, will usually increase more rapidly than if the system remained closed.[3]

The results of the 2nd Law of Thermodynamics are evident everywhere in our world and its effects are observed in basically all aspects of our lives. It seems that everything in nature tends to decay or become more disorganized over time. In "Second Law of Thermodynamics: Does This Basic Law of Nature Prevent Evolution?" Paul S. Taylor writes this:

Everything ages and wears out. Even death is a manifestation of this law. The effects of the 2nd Law are all around, touching everything in the universe.[4]

As discussed earlier, the proponents of evolution maintain that random chance mutations and natural selection over long periods of time yield species of organisms that are more complex and organized and thus more fit for survival. However, Taylor also goes on to say this:

In the long run, complex, ordered arrangements actually tend to become simpler and more disorderly with time. There is an irreversible downward trend ultimately at work throughout the universe. Evolution, with its ever increasing order and complexity, appears impossible in the natural world.[5]

I realize that I've cited only a couple of opinions, but they make sense to me. Just look around. Everything we observe in nature seems to follow this pattern of increasing chaos and decay, so why would I disregard this evidence in favor of a theory? Give me real observations over pure theory anytime.

Complexity of DNA

Most everyone has heard of DNA tests that allow us to determine what regions of the world our ancestors were from. As we see on television, law enforcement can conduct DNA testing of blood samples collected at the scene of a crime to help identify the people involved in that crime. Test results from these samples are so precise that they can be used as admissible evidence in a court of law. The reason they can do that is that every person has a unique DNA pattern.

As we all learned in high school biology class, DNA is the chemical substance that makes up the genes that form the chromosome pairs that reside in the nuclei of our cells, and these chromosomes determine the characteristics of a person. Anyone with a basic knowledge of DNA will attest that the structure of the chromosomes and their genes and the mechanism in which they determine the characteristics of a human are extremely complex. Only in the past few years have brilliant researchers figured all this out. Could anyone honestly believe it is possible for such a system to evolve with all its complexity by random chance mutations and natural selection, given the efforts of these brilliant researchers over the years?

Creation of the First Cell

A living cell consists of many components that must work together through complex processes to survive and function. Biologists and microbiologists from around the world have been trying for years to create a living cell, and they have made tremendous advances in this effort. But, to my knowledge, they have not yet created a single living cell from only inorganic chemicals that can live and reproduce on its own. Could anyone honestly believe a living cell was created by random chance, considering the efforts of these brilliant scientists over many years?

Even if these scientists were eventually successful, I still must question where the inorganic matter they used came from? The Bible says that God created man from the dust of the earth. I recall a joke in which some atheists told God that they, too, could create a living being. But when they reached down and grabbed some dust from the earth, God quickly told them, "No, that's mine. Use your own material."

Origins of Appendages/Organs

A major point of contention for me concerning evolution is how mutations initiate the development of various useful appendages or organs in an animal species. Good examples would be wings or eyes, as we will discuss later. I agree that a few cells may develop as a mutation, but an appendage or organ would have to develop to such an extent that it would be useful to the species to promote evolution for enhanced development, and how could it ever get to that point through random mutations and natural selection? In the early stages of development, what would initiate enhanced development with the addition of a few more cells? It would be impossible for a useful organ or appendage to have been conceptualized for further development through early stages of evolution, for there would have been no goal to pursue.

Birds and certain insects have the unique ability to fly, but how did their wings evolve? If birds evolved from another species without wings, it seems that the first mutations from its ancestor toward this end would have to start the development of both wings simultaneously, and that seems unlikely. A complete set of wings is required for flight; a single partially developed wing would serve no purpose at all. The odds of two perfectly symmetrical wings developing by chance mutations simultaneously on the species are infinitesimal.

Complexity of the Human Body

The human body is so complex that even after all these years, medical researchers learn more about it every day. Just think of the body's systems: skeletal, muscular, circulatory, respiratory, nervous, digestive, endocrine, lymphatic, excretory, renal, and so on. The systems are so complex that physician specialists limit their practice to just one, so that we can go to a urologist, cardiologist, neurologist, gastroenterologist, or orthopedic physician, to name just a few. These physicians are required to have several years of training in their specialty beyond the requirements for a general practitioner.

Each system has many complex components that must work together to allow the system, and thus the entire body, to function properly. If any component fails, the whole system can become severely degraded or even fail. Likewise, if any systems fail, the whole body is severely degraded or may fail. I find it difficult to believe that all these complex systems developed to interact perfectly inside the human body by evolving from a single cell. In the next three sections, I discuss three of these systems, at a very basic level, that most of us learned about in school and/or because of health problems of our own or someone close to us.

The Circulatory System

The circulatory system includes, along with the heart, thousands of miles of blood vessels consisting of veins, arteries, and capillaries, as well as the blood they transport. Blood carries the nutrients and oxygen required by all organs and tissues of the body and provides for elimination of wastes from these tissues and organs. Arteries carry blood rich in oxygen to the organs and tissues, and veins transport blood low in oxygen back to the heart. Blood is replenished with oxygen via the lungs. Capillaries are small blood vessels that transport blood between arteries, veins, and cells.

The heart is an organ made of muscle and chambers that pump blood through the circulatory system. Heartbeats result from nerve impulses from the SA node in the right atrium of the heart, which causes the heart chambers to alternately contract, thus forcing blood throughout the circulatory system. The heart muscle alternately contracts and relaxes nonstop twenty-four hours a day, seven days a week, for your entire life to circulate blood throughout the body through the arteries, veins, and capillaries.

Suppose a person lives to be seventy years old and that on average their heart beats seventy times per minute. There are sixty minutes in an hour, twenty-four hours in a day, and about 365.25 days in a year, so if we multiply seventy heartbeats by sixty minutes by twenty-four hours by 365.25 days by seventy years, we obtain approximately 2,577,204,000 heartbeats in the life of a seventy-year-old person. That is more than 2.5 billion heartbeats continuously without stopping for a rest. The heart would beat nonstop from a few days after conception until the person was seventy years old, and that is a long time. How could that organ have just evolved to function nonstop, so efficiently, and for so long?

The circulatory system—the heart with its four chambers, arteries, veins, capillaries, blood, and other components—is complex and extensive, running throughout the entire body. Look at how perfect the composition of the blood is that contains all the things necessary to transport the required nutrients to all the tissues of the body and provide for the elimination of wastes from them.

It appears that the circulatory system must have been designed and put in place all at once, rather than through an evolutionary process, because none of the components would be any good without the others. Also none of the other systems of the body could function without this entire circulatory system in place. For the entire body to function, the circulatory system had to have been developed simultaneously with all the other systems and organs. How could evolution, through random mutations and natural selection, have created such a complex, integrated entity?

The Neurological System

The neurological system consists of the brain and nerves, which permeate the entire body. The brain controls the body by sending nerve impulses through the spinal cord and then on to the tissues of the body to direct their functions. Some functions are automatic whereas others are voluntary. The human brain is the most sophisticated thing, living or nonliving, that has ever existed. Even highly developed computers pale in comparison to the human brain, or even the brain of most any animal, for that matter. Remember, it took a human brain to develop a computer. A computer has basically memory and logic, and this logic was programmed. Even artificial intelligence software was programmed, giving it the ability to imitate certain limited basic human behavior, such as image recognition, or basic decision making for some predetermined process. Compare that to a brain that provides the mechanisms for thought, reasoning, logic, memory, and can experience all five senses (sight, hearing, taste, touch, smell) as well as experiencing the emotions (happiness, sadness, fear, anger).

Like the circulatory system, the neurological system, which is necessary for the function of all other organs and systems, is such an extensive, complex network that it would had to have been designed and not a result of evolution. A RadioTimes.com article titled "Secrets of the Brain" puts all this into perspective: "'If I gave you a hundred billion pieces of Lego with pulleys and levers,' says David Eagleman, 'and you hooked up this incredibly complex system and set it going, at what point do you say: Okay now it's experiencing the taste of feta cheese?' The American neuroscientist is explaining that despite remarkable recent advances in the fields of robotics and computer science we are unlikely to ever invent a machine as complex as the human brain."[6]

The Digestive System

Every cell of the body requires nutrition. Food taken into the body is broken down as it travels through the digestive tract, and the nutrients are removed from the food and sent to the cells. This process involves the mouth, esophagus, stomach, small intestine, large intestine, and other organs. Muscles move food through the system, and juices and enzymes are provided by the stomach, pancreas, liver, and the small intestine to break down food as it travels through the digestive tract. The circulatory system carries digested nutrients from the small intestine to the cells, whose waste products are carried by the bloodstream for excretion from the body.

Thus we see that many organs, systems, and processes are involved in a tremendously complex process to make nutrition happen. None of the components would be of any use without the others, which suggests that they would all have to be in place from the beginning.

Looking at these three systems—circulatory, neurological, and digestive—we see how they all need to be in place and fully functional, for they are dependent upon one another. I cannot comprehend how such an extensive, complex, and fully integrated set of interdependent systems could have developed from random chance mutations and natural selection.

Healing and Rejuvenation of the Human Body

The human body has an inherent ability to heal itself from injury and disease. The structure of each cell is determined by its DNA, and when a cell is damaged, certain body processes go into immediate action to repair the structure of the cell and return it to normal. They even create new cells as needed to facilitate the healing. Watching our bodies heal, we don't fully comprehend the complex biological processes taking place behind the scene.

In addition to repairing itself from injuries and diseases, the body continually replaces its older cells, worn out from everyday wear and tear, by generating new cells. In contrast, I'm not aware of any engineer or scientist who has ever come close to making something that can continually repair and rejuvenate itself. I wish they could, because it would be nice to own a car, or anything else for that matter, that could repair itself.

It is astounding how the body can do this miraculous work, and most people don't realize how complex and intricate this process really is. It would take a highly trained physician or scientist with expertise in biology, microbiology, genetics, etc. to describe all the components and complex processes involved in this magnificent healing and rejuvenation process. It is beyond comprehension that the human body, which can repair and rejuvenate itself and survive for many years, could be developed by evolution through random chance mutations and natural selection.

Human Emotions

Humans have emotions such as love, happiness, sadness, anger, fear, and surprise. These emotions manifest themselves from time to time in most people, usually resulting from life's situations. Advanced animal species, such as cats and dogs, display similar emotions. Love is one of the most powerful emotions that humans and most animal species experience for others such as family and friends. Look at how pets love their masters and how many will go to great lengths to protect them from harm.

If our bodies were only biological—not spiritual—it would seem impossible for all these emotions to have evolved to the extent that they manifest themselves. Emotions such as love are so strong that most parents would give their lives for their children without hesitation. This implies the existence of a soul created by God.

Darwin Discusses Possible Difficulties with His Theory of Evolution

As you probably have realized by now, I reject the theory that a species can evolve into a more advanced species through random chance mutations and natural selection. Instead, I believe all the various species of animals and plants resulted from a creator. In looking for evidences to support my view, I began to read Charles Darwin's book *On the Origin of Species*.

As I looked through the table of contents, I saw that chapter 6 was titled "Difficulties on Theory." This certainly got my attention, and I immediately began to read chapter 6, which begins with the following quote by Darwin:

"Long before having arrived at this part of my work, a crowd of difficulties will have occurred to the reader. Some of them are so grave that to this day I can never reflect on them without being staggered;"[7]

Darwin immediately goes on to mention four serious problems with his theory of evolution. However, it is highly unlikely that you would hear these problems presented in a science class, despite the fact that Darwin admits that these difficulties pose a real problem for his theory. In the same chapter, he attempts to show how each one of the four difficulties he mentions could possibly somehow be justified through random chance mutations and natural selection. I want to mention three of those difficulties, the first of which concerns transitional forms:

"Firstly, why, if species have descended from other species by insensibly fine gradations, do we not everywhere see innumerable transitional forms? Why is not all nature in confusion instead of the species being, as we see them, well defined?"[8]

In this passage, Darwin says plainly that if evolution were valid, we should see countless numbers of verifiable transitional forms. We should expect to see these transitional forms throughout the world, if species gradually change from one species to another.

Some evolutionists may disagree, but I believe that archeologists have never documented a species that is, without any doubt, a transitional form between two different species. Even Darwin, the father of evolution, says that each species seems to be well defined, rather than part one species and part another. Darwin was born more than two hundred years ago, so there has been adequate time to find the transitional forms that he claimed should exist if evolution were true.

Darwin next questions how an animal species could be formed with different structure and habits from another species through evolution:

> "Secondly, is it possible that an animal having, for instance, the structure and habits of a bat, could have been formed by the modification of some other animal with wholly different habits?"[9]

Then he goes on to question the evolution of instincts in animals:

> "Thirdly, can instincts be acquired and modified through natural selection? What shall we say to so marvelous an instinct as that which leads the bee to make cells, which have practically anticipated the discoveries of profound mathematicians?"[10]

These two difficulties will be discussed further in the next chapter.

Six

A Designer Is Required

I'm sure you have heard the familiar phrase "Stop and smell the roses." Take a moment and just look around at the beauty in our world. Note the many kinds of plants and animals, each with its own characteristics and specific function. See how the different things in our world depend on and interact with each other for the total world to function.

Have you ever wondered how evolution could explain this? In my opinion, the complex, marvelous designs in nature are among the best scientific evidence for our God. Nature's marvelous designs are too perfect to have come about through random chance and natural selection. I believe that nature provides vast amounts of evidence that a personal designer was responsible for these miraculous, complex designs and their interdependent relationships. The following sections present situations that demonstrate the necessity of a designer. There are unlimited numbers of examples, but we'll restrict our discussion to just a few.

Basic Building Blocks of Nature

In chapter 4 we discussed how atoms, the basic building blocks of matter, are complex objects consisting of elementary particles (protons, neutrons, electrons, and others) in various numbers and configurations. By what mechanism did these particles become configured to form atoms, which bond to form the different types of molecules that compose matter? If all the different atoms were eternally present, it would still require a designer to put the complex mechanisms into place to produce the required molecules that form complex substances.

Inherent Natural Instincts of Animals

Common to most animal species are inherent instincts such as survival, protecting their young from predators, acquiring food, and so on. In addition, each species has unique instincts that benefit it in its own environment. Instincts must be the result of a designer at work, for there is no other explanation for the many natural instincts that we observe in nature. As we discussed in chapter 5, in *On the Origin of Species*, Darwin himself questioned how instincts could have evolved.

Honeybees possess the ability to construct almost perfect hexagonal honeycomb cells that always fit together perfectly, and they build these perfect designs without any tools. Darwin mentions this in *On the Origin of Species*, as discussed in chapter 5. Hornets as well as other wasps also possess this ability.

The bodies of spiders are equipped to create sophisticated webs to trap their prey. Did the body equipment to produce the webs and the inherent instincts to create the webs come about simultaneously through random chance mutations? Or did evolution first equip the spiders with the ability to make webs and then teach them how to use webs to trap their prey? In either case, how was the whole concept conceived of in the first place?

Go outside on a warm spring day and you can hear birds chirping and singing. They have varied beautiful colors, and each type has its own unique sound as they seem happy. I have a birdbath in my yard where I see robins, redbirds, doves, and other beautiful birds drinking water and flapping their wings to bathe themselves.

I am convinced by their actions that they know the birdbath is there specifically for them. I wonder why I never see unwanted scavenger birds such as crows and buzzards drinking water from the birdbath. Look at how groups of birds know that flying in a V-shaped configuration will maximize their flight efficiency, and the lead bird is spelled by another bird when the lead bird gets tired. I marvel at the guidance mechanism birds have that allows them to migrate south in the winter and return to their original place of habitation in the spring.

Observe how birds and squirrels prepare nests in trees to raise their young. Birds protect and feed their baby birds as they grow, but push them out of the nest when it's time for them to fly. Was this knowledge obtained through evolution, or was it given to them by God? Squirrels know they must store food for winter, and they know to build their nests in trees so other animals won't bother their young.

Doves are portrayed as special creatures in the Bible. Unlike most other species, doves tend to pair up for life, male and female, much like humans. Rarely do you see a single dove. This instinct to mate for life is rare among animal species. If it arose through evolution, why isn't it found in many other species? It seems to me that doves got this instinct from their designer.

I see mother cats move kittens around by the napes of their necks. How do they instinctively know that this won't choke the kitten, as I would have first thought? As with most mammals, kittens know to suck milk from their mothers. How did this knowledge come about? Was it taught to them or is it instinctual?

I have owned several dogs as pets over the years and thus I'm familiar with the species. I am amazed at their abilities and instincts. For instance, dogs such as border collies can understand many words so well that sometimes we have to spell words that we don't want them to hear. This probably results from word association, but it is still impressive because of the significant number of words they can learn to recognize. Many dogs have great personalities, and they're not scared when we play energetically with them. On a lighter note, it is amusing how dogs often bury bones so that no person or other animal can get them.

Most pets have endearing love for their masters. Many seem to know when their beloved master is sick, and sometimes they will try to get help if their master is incapacitated. Many cats and dogs will go to great extremes to protect their master or to rescue them from harm. This emotion of love is not learned, but was instilled in them by their designer, and this is just a small sample of examples that could be mentioned.

Diversity of Animal Species

Look at the diversity of animal species on earth and think about how different they are—humans, bees, snakes, birds, horses, cows, mice, fleas, flies, dogs, cats, elephants, giraffes, alligators, fish, turtles, and so on. They exhibit great diversity in appearance and abilities. Animals such as oxen and elephants have great size and strength, and others such as tigers and lions are ferocious in pursuing their prey. Leopards and greyhounds have great speed, and turtles and snails are slow. Birds and certain insects fly, fish swim and live in water, and snakes and certain worms slither. Regardless, evolutionists believe they're all related through a common ancestor.

Animals such as turtles and snails have a protective shell to protect them from predators. These shells appear to be fully integrated with the rest of the animal's body, rather than just appendages, because snails and turtles can't survive without their shells. These shelled species are different from other species in this regard, so what species could be their ancestors? Have we uncovered any precursor transitional forms for these shelled species?

Aquatic species—fish, whales, sharks, lobsters, shrimp, starfish, and so on—are equipped to function and survive only in water. What is their relation to land creatures with respect to evolution? Each species seems designed for its own specific environment. What would be the benefit, through natural selection, of an aquatic species evolving into a land species, or vice versa?

Snakes must slither along the ground using muscles that allow them to move from side to side. This is different from other land species that use legs to move about. What would be the probability that random chance mutations and natural selection would yield species with such different methods of mobility?

Various animal species possess different numbers of legs. Snakes and earthworms have none, birds and humans have two, most reptiles such as horses and cows have four, most insects have six, and so on. How could evolution result in differing numbers of legs in various species?

Skunks spray a noxious odor, intolerable to most other species, at anything they perceive as an enemy, and porcupines have sharp quills covering their bodies to protect them from their enemies. These highly developed mechanisms for self-protection are rare among animal species. Would we expect them to result from random chance mutations and natural selection and thus have precursor transitional forms?

Dogs have senses far superior to those of humans. Some have a sense of smell so sensitive that they can be used to track down criminals or even children who may have wandered away from home. Dogs are used by the police to detect hidden illegal drugs, and guard dogs have a sense of hearing so acute that they can hear the slightest of noises made by an unwanted intruder. The human species is far superior to all other species, so why would humans not have these same abilities as a result of evolution?

I find it extremely difficult to entertain the idea that certain species could be related via evolution—bumblebees and snakes, houseflies and giraffes, fish and cows, fleas and elephants, and so on. The standard answer would be that they have common ancestors, but that would require an incredible degree of diverse evolution to take place. It just doesn't seem possible to me for all that to transpire.

It is inconceivable to me how evolution could lead from a single living cell to all these diverse species. Remember, Charles Darwin himself questioned how evolution could lead to such great diversity. If you believe it, then you certainly have more faith—though not *Christian* faith—than I do. It seems more reasonable that a designer developed this huge variety of unique creatures.

Varieties of Insects

There are many varieties of insects, which I'll discuss separately from other animals because of their small size. Flies, wasps, and bees can fly; some insects walk on tiny legs; and still others can both fly and walk.

I fondly remember being a child and trying to catch lightning bugs in the summer night. Lightning bugs are fascinating because they light up to attract mates. They can cause chemical reactions to occur in their bodies that make them glow. It seems totally impossible to me that random mutations and natural selection afforded them this ability. What species could possibly be their precursor?

Ant hills show up in my yard from time to time. Each hill is made of sand that the ants bring to the surface as they create tunnels underground. Ants form colonies, each with a queen and worker ants, and each colony functions as a small community in which the ants work together for a common purpose. This involve a fairly high level of sophistication among the ants—communication, organization, and cooperation—to accomplish their common goals. A few other insects such as bees and termites also colonize. This propensity for colonization is strong among the ant population, though rare for other animal species, so how could it result from natural selection?

There are hundreds of varieties of beautiful butterflies, and many cities have butterfly houses where you can see butterflies on display. Their wings vary in design and color, so how could natural selection yield all these different butterflies with their beautiful colors?

Many insects, such as bees and butterflies, have wings that allow them to fly, but so do birds. How could a small winged insect be related via evolution to much larger birds through a common ancestor, or did wings just happen to evolve independently for each of them? How could two different species with such extreme size differences just happen to both evolve wings that allow them both to fly?

The various species of insects are so diverse in appearance and function that it is inconceivable to me how they could have evolved from a common ancestor. The vast diversity among the various species is an argument against evolution from a common ancestor, whereas the commonalities suggest that a designer was intimately at work in their creation.

Varieties of Plants

Look at all the varieties of plants and trees, which vary in shape, size, and appearance. They have the required structures and capabilities to take in water and minerals and use carbon dioxide to live and grow. Like animals, these capabilities, even at the cellular level, are extremely complex. Did all these different plants originate from a single plant cell through evolution, or were they designed separately? How did the first plant cell get all its required components evolved and put into place for it to function as a living cell? By what mechanism did this first cell develop the intelligence to divide, thus promoting growth to create the first complete plant?

If evolution is responsible, why are magnolia trees so different from pine trees when they live in the same environment? That question can be asked about all the other vastly diverse plants and trees that coexist under similar conditions. I don't see how natural selection was at work here.

Most Plants Require Seeds for Procreation

Most plants reproduce through the production of seeds, which have all the information necessary to grow a new plant similar to its parent. For plants to procreate, all this structure would have to be in place from the start, beginning with the first plant that existed. Some plants procreate through spores, but that too involves a complex process that seems to require a designer at work.

Beautiful Flowers and Pollination

I enjoy all types of beautiful flowers—roses, violets, azaleas, petunias, daffodils, orchids, marigolds, daises, carnations, geraniums, pansies, buttercups, impatiens, morning glories, sunflowers, tulips, lilies, and so on. The various colors and perfectly symmetrical arrangements of petals, stems, and leaves are so beautiful, and many flowers also have nice fragrances. In my wildest dreams, I cannot imagine how things so beautiful and perfect could develop randomly without a designer. What role would natural selection play in producing all these beautiful flowers?

Bees collect nectar and pollen from flowers and carry the pollen to other flowers to fertilize them. Many plants would have a difficult time surviving without bees to help with pollination. When a bee collects nectar from a flower, pollen from the stamen (male reproductive organ) sticks to the bee. When this bee goes to the next flower, some of this pollen is transferred to the pistil (female reproductive organ). Wind can also carry pollen from flower to flower. This is how the required fertilization takes place.

What are the odds that both the stamen and pistil would evolve at the same time through random chance mutations to accomplish fertilization in flowers? One would be useless without the other. When did the evolutionary process determine that bees are useful in pollination? It seems impossible that all this complex perfect structure and process could be developed through evolution.

Fibonacci Sequence

One of the most intriguing sets of numbers is the Fibonacci sequence, named after a twelfth-century Italian mathematician. The Fibonacci sequence is 0, 1, 1, 2, 3, 5, 8, 13, 21, 34, 55, and so on to infinity. Beginning with the third number, each subsequent number is the sum of the two previous numbers. The Fibonacci sequence, beginning at 2, seems to be the blueprint for many designs found widespread in nature. The ratio of each number to the previous number is approximately 1.6, a ratio that occurs so often in nature that it is hard to fathom that it could be coincidental.

Many plants and flowers exhibit the Fibonacci sequence in their structures through their leaf arrangements and number of petals. There are many spirals in nature, such as snails, seashells, spiral galaxies, and more whose basic structures are based on the Fibonacci sequence. In class, I have used the Fibonacci sequence of numbers to draw such spirals.

The lengths of the bones in human fingers and wrists, beginning at the fingertips, have ratios that fit the Fibonacci sequence of 2, 3, 5, 8. Starting at the fingertips, the successive adjacent bones get longer by approximately the Fibonacci sequence. I could cite many more examples, but the existence of something as precise as the Fibonacci sequence, appearing so prominently in nature, suggests that it didn't happen by random chance. It suggests to me that someone had to be intimately involved with a design plan.

Exquisite Design of the Earth and Universe

On a clear night, I look at the sky and recollect what I studied in astronomy in college. I see the stars and realize the vastness of our universe with all its galaxies. Our own star, the sun, provides the light needed for our survival and for plants to survive using photosynthesis.

The sun, moon, and earth have relative sizes and are relatively positioned to provide a suitable climate on earth to adequately sustain life. Look at how the earth tilts on its axis as it rotates around the sun to produce the necessary seasons. The earth spins on its axis to produce days and nights of just the required length for our survival. Day is required for our sun to give its essential rays for life, and night is required for the earth to refresh itself. In *The Creator and the Cosmos*, Ross says this about the earth's rotation: "If the planet takes too long to rotate, temperature differences between day and night will be too great. On the other hand, if the planet rotates too rapidly, wind velocities will rise to catastrophic levels."[1]

Ross gives this excellent summary: "So we see that Earth is prepared for life through a variety of finely tuned characteristics of our galaxy, star, planet, and moon."[2] It seems to me that all this had to have been designed and put into place by a supernatural power.

Hydrologic Water Cycle

Many grade school science textbooks teach the hydrologic water cycle, which is perfect in its purpose of supplying water to all things on earth that depend upon it. Water on the surface of the earth becomes heated and evaporates to form water vapor and thus clouds in the air. The wind carries these clouds to various parts of the earth. The moisture in the clouds later cools and rain is produced, which supplies the earth and its inhabitants with water.

This perfect water cycle is perpetually repeated, over and over. Without this ever-occurring perfect water cycle, all life on earth would disappear. I have a hunch about how this system came about and was put into place from the beginning.

Complex Organs

People who believe in creation frequently ask how the complex organs of the human body could have developed through evolution. Most organs must be fully developed before they can function at all, so a partially developed organ would seem to be of little use.

The organs most commonly considered in this discussion are the eyes of a human. If eyes are the result of evolution, then an early intermediate form of the species would have possessed no eyes. At what point and by what mechanism during the evolution of the species did the species sense that light existed? When was it determined that a functioning eye required a lens, retina, nerves, and so on? A transparent lens is needed to gather light and transmit it to the retina. Light receptors would have to develop on the retina to sense the light, nerves had to develop to transmit the light impulses from the retina to the brain, and the brain had to be able to logically make sense of the light. And when was it determined that two eyes are needed for good depth perception?

It seems that the whole eye had to have been conceptualized and designed from the beginning for all the required components to be put into place. In my logical mind, there is no other reasonable alternative.

Development of Opposite Sexes

How was the development of opposite sexes in a species possible without design? Note how complex and different are the structure and function of the reproductive organs of both the male and female of a species, while still complementing each other perfectly in the reproductive process. How could the process of evolution determine that an organism needed an opposite-sex partner to produce offspring and initiate such development?

If reproduction was initially asexual, meaning that an organism could divide and reproduce by itself without an opposite-sex partner, when and by what mechanism did the development of the opposite sex commence? It seems absurd that anyone could believe these perfect mates could have resulted simultaneously through random chance mutations and natural selection.

As previously mentioned, plants also have male and female organs that are required for fertilization. By what mechanism did plants determine they required both male and female organs that perfectly complemented each other for fertilization to take place? And how was it decided that something like a bee was needed to facilitate this reproductive process through pollination? This suggests that these organs had to be developed concurrently by a designer with a plan to put all this into place.

Human Birth

Human birth is one of the most beautiful, amazing, and intriguing things in life, but most people have no inkling of the complexity of the many underlying biological processes that must occur at each stage, all the way from conception to the actual birth of a child. I believe that all this must be a miracle from God.

First, as previously discussed, both the male and female had to develop with just the right reproductive parts that complemented each other to allow reproduction to occur. A sperm cell from a male and an egg from a female must come together to start the development of the fetus. The fetus must develop and be nurtured through the facilities of the female. During a nine-month period, a beautifully complete human being with all its organs and systems is developed. During this time, the fetus is totally dependent upon the mother to live and carry on its bodily functions.

Then there is birth, in which the baby becomes a fully functioning living being all on its own, relatively independent of its mother for survival. From the moment of birth, an infant must breathe and perform all other bodily functions on its own. What an amazing turn of events! Can you imagine how evolution could lead to this process? The creation of a baby requires so many processes that must take place along the way that it is inconceivable to me how all this could happen without having been designed.

We could go on and on with examples that lend support for a creator and designer. There are many articles written by experts in various scientific fields that you can read for much further in-depth technical discussion in this subject area.

Creator Had Personal Interest in Man

The design of the universe makes it clear that the eternal creator had a personal interest in man. He created the world with all its beauty and gave humans earthly domain over it, as the Bible says. He gave us superior intelligence and thus dominance over all other creatures on earth. No other creature even comes close intellectually to humans. Look at all the things He provided to humans that only we can enjoy. God didn't have to create humans—or anything else, for that matter—but He did. Do we just take that for granted?

Seven

Chance Experiences?

In this chapter, I describe personal experiences that many people would ascribe to chance or coincidence. However, these experiences defy logical explanation, and I believe they are the result of a caring, personal, higher authority. Permission to discuss the experiences was obtained from those involved, or from a close family member for those who are deceased. I know of many such experiences from family, close friends, and others, but only a small sample can be given here as examples.

* * * * *

When I was young, my mother used an extension cord to plug in the iron while ironing clothes. If she had to interrupt her ironing to attend to something, she would sometimes just unplug the iron from the extension cord, leaving the extension cord plugged into the electrical outlet.

Like other babies, I would crawl around and put whatever I found into my mouth. One day an FBI investigator came to our home; he was doing a background investigation on a former student of my dad's. Dad was not home, so my mother, who was ironing at the time, unplugged the iron from the extension cord and went into another room to talk with him. A few minutes later, the FBI agent heard a frying sound and rushed into the room where my mother had been ironing. The end of the extension cord was in my mouth, and I was being electrocuted. He jerked the extension cord from my mouth, and they rushed me to the doctor in our local town. That doctor said he couldn't do anything for me, so they took me as fast as they could to another town about twenty miles away, where there was a hospital. The FBI agent turned his siren on and drove about 100 mph to get me there. According to my mother, I almost died—and would have if the FBI agent hadn't been there to help.

I don't think it was a coincidence that the FBI agent was there when I put that extension cord in my mouth. I believe he was an angel whom God put in that situation for me. Because my mother often left that extension cord plugged in, an accident was destined to happen sooner or later, and it could have happened at a time when that FBI agent wasn't there.

* * * * *

I have written thousands of checks on my bank accounts over the years. Because of unfortunate circumstances several years ago, I was living from paycheck to paycheck. One Sunday morning as I was getting ready for church, I was trying to decide whether I could give some money to the church that day. I was low on funds and wouldn't get paid until a week or so later. After extensive thought and prayer, I finally decided to give a small amount, so I wrote a check and placed it in the collection plate at church.

When I received my bank statement at the end of the month, that check was among the canceled checks, indicating that the church had received the money. However, as I tried to balance my checkbook, I discovered that the amount of that check had not been taken from my account. Wanting to correct the error, I called the bank and told them about it. They said not to worry, for the balance on my next monthly statement would be adjusted to account for the check.

The next monthly statement, however, didn't account for that check. I called the bank again, and they again assured me that it would be corrected on the following monthly statement. When that third statement still didn't account for the check, I decided that I had done my best to correct the error, which involved only a small amount of money anyway.

To this day, it is as though I never wrote that check, even though the church obtained the money. In all my years of writing checks, this is the only time a check has not been accounted for. What are the odds of this happening at all, much less for that specific check that I had prayed over whether to write? I believe God was saying that if I put my trust in Him, everything would be okay.

* * * * *

One Friday afternoon, an acquaintance stopped by my house and told me they didn't have any money. They wouldn't get paid until the following Tuesday, and they needed to buy gasoline and groceries. They knew I played golf, so they had brought a couple of clubs and asked if I would be interested in buying them. I had recently bought a new set of golf clubs, but I knew they were sincere, so I just gave them a small amount of money to help them get by until the following week.

About five months earlier, I had stopped by an ATM and withdrew money from my checking account. Since I was not going home right away, I locked the money—several loose twenty-dollar bills—and withdrawal slip in the pocket of my car. My life was hectic during that time, and I then forgot all about the money. Since stopping at that ATM, I had opened that pocket at least twenty times—and although it seems impossible, I never noticed the money or withdrawal slip. But then, a couple of days after I helped the person described above, there it was in plain sight—ten times as much money as I had given to them.

I later shared with the other person involved all that had transpired, and we rejoiced together knowing that God had shown us that when we help someone in need, He will reward us many times over. I truly believe that God planned that situation as a lesson for me from the beginning.

* * * * *

A dear friend of mine had breast surgery for cancer many years ago when she was still young. The doctor told her that if the cancer didn't return within five years, she would be considered cured. Over the years, even though she showed no indication of recurrence, she continued to worry that the cancer would return. Eventually her anxiety began interfering with her ability to live a normal life.

She was a devout Christian, and one night as she lay in bed praying about her condition, she said she believes the Lord literally spoke to her and said that she would be made whole. From that moment, she didn't worry about cancer. She is over ninety years old now, and the cancer has never returned.

* * * * *

One day a friend of mine was washing the top of his large boat, he slipped and fell almost twelve feet to the deck below, landing flat on his back. As he was falling, however, it felt like he was floating slowly downward, as though an angel were lowering him slowly and carefully to the deck. He said it was just like someone laying a baby in its bassinet.

He immediately jumped up without any problem—no injuries whatsoever. Realistically he should have been hurt badly, having broken several bones or possibly even been killed, considering the distance he fell and the hard deck he landed on. He believes an angel had been looking over him.

* * * * *

A young friend of mine was taking the pitcher's mound to pitch for his college baseball team, when he noticed his great-grandmother standing behind his dad in the crowd. Even though she was in her nineties, she looked young, was dressed nicely, and had a big smile on her face. She had often said that she hoped to see him play college baseball someday. He immediately became distraught, stepped off the pitcher's mound, and knelt and began to pray—to the amazement of everyone there.

When he stepped back on the mound, he could no longer see his great-grandmother. She had died the previous day, but the family hadn't told him. They had wanted to wait until after the game, because scouts for professional teams planned to be there to watch him play. After the game, the young man went straight to his dad and told him that he knew his great-grandmother had died. What an amazing testimony showing how God works.

* * * * *

My daughter left a good job to take another job that offered more potential for career advancement. After a few weeks, because of certain circumstances at her new job, she started questioning whether she had done the right thing. Then she had a chance meeting with a personable man during an event associated with her job. Without knowing anything about my daughter's situation, he told her that it was on his heart to tell her that she was right where she was supposed to be. She had been called, and God was going to use her job to have an influence on other people's lives.

He told her that he was a minister and that sometimes God would lead him to deliver messages to people. My daughter believes that God used him to encourage her, and now that some time has passed, it appears the message he relayed to her provided good advice.

* * * * *

My grandmother was in the local nursing home, but she seemed to be doing well. Her husband—my grandfather—had died of lung cancer at least thirty years earlier, when I was about five years old. I have vivid memories of him in great agony as he struggled to breathe during those last few days as he was dying. He was a great man and Christian, and everyone who knew him loved him.

One night, a close relative dreamed that my grandmother was waiting outside by the highway with her luggage. In her dream, a bus stopped, my grandfather got off and helped my grandmother, along with her luggage, onto the bus, and then the bus drove off. The next morning, she was disturbed and told the family about the dream. Shortly afterward, the family received a phone call that my grandmother was dying. I believe that God used that dream to tell us that my grandmother was going to heaven to be with my grandfather.

* * * * *

For a few years, I attended the singles Sunday school class at our church. Two good friends of mine were in that class, and they started dating and eventually married. They were a happy Christian couple, but a few years later, the husband fell ill from cancer. His wife tells that on the day he died, he had been lying in bed unconscious and hadn't moved in five days. That morning, she was in the bedroom taking care of him. Suddenly he raised his arms into the air, and with a great big smile on his face, he passed away. His wife is convinced that he saw heavenly angels or even Jesus calling him home.

* * * * *

I had a good Christian friend with whom I attended a weekly Bible study class. He enjoyed riding his motorcycle, and he told the group of an experience he had one rainy night when his motorcycle had run off a road in the middle of nowhere. Although he had been thrown from the motorcycle, it had felt like he was flying through the air in slow motion, and he had not been badly hurt. Even though it was a remote rural place, someone wearing a raincoat appeared and asked if he was okay. As others arrived to help, my friend asked if anyone had seen that person, but no one had. He believes it was an angel who witnessed the accident and prevented him from getting hurt badly—or maybe even prevented his death.

* * * * *

I know of a hospice nurse who on many occasions personally witnessed to people who are dying. Many seemed filled with great joy and appeared to see someone not visible to anyone else in the room. She believes those beings were probably angels coming to escort these believers to heaven. However, other people seemed to be in much distress as they died, screaming that they were hot or their feet were burning. The hospice nurse said she believed these people were not saved. She had tried to witness to them, but without much success.

* * * * *

A friend recently told me a truly amazing and inspiring experience he had. He was watching television with his family and they observed that he had lost consciousness. They took him to the local hospital where it was determined that he had a subdural hematoma. The doctors performed brain surgery and he was soon able to go home. After some time he was having difficulty breathing, and he returned to the hospital and remained there for a couple of weeks but was not getting any better.

He was then transferred to a major hospital with a great reputation that had a medical school. He was diagnosed as having antiphospholipid syndrome with blood clots in both legs, both lungs, and kidneys. His legs were extremely swollen, and he was placed on blood thinners. His family had great concern for they didn't know whether he would live or die.

After about five weeks the swelling in his legs went down, and the doctors were ready for him to try to get up and walk. The next three days they had him sit up on the edge of the bed and just dangle his legs. After that it was time for him to stand on his feet and try to walk. However, his legs would not straighten out thus prohibiting him from being able to stand. So he told them to just lay him back in the bed. He was totally devastated.

Being down in the dumps over his situation he wanted to read something comforting. So, that night he picked up the Gideon Bible that was there in the hospital room. With no particular book, chapter, or verse of the Bible in mind, he just happened to open it and began reading starting at Hebrews 12:12. Hebrews 12:12,13 says, "Wherefore lift up the hands which hang down, and the feeble knees; And make straight paths for your feet, lest that which is lame be turned out of the way; but let it rather be healed."

The very next day my friend was able to get out of bed and start walking. He steadily progressed back to good health from that day on. What an amazing testimony in support of our God.

I can attest that all the experiences I have discussed actually happened. I talked to most of the participants directly, and others relayed their experiences to close family members of mine. One might say that these were chance occurrences, but without considering the existence of a supernatural God, how can we account for the hundreds of such experiences that happen to people every day?

Part Three

The Bible, Inspired Word of God

Eight

The Bible: Its Survival and Harmony

The survival of the Bible itself certainly supports its authenticity. In "The Preservation of the Bible," Mike Matthews writes, "One of the most amazing testimonies to Scripture's truth is its preservation over thousands of years despite sometimes intense efforts to destroy it."[1] Matthews cites specific efforts to destroy the Bible: "In 175 BC the king of Syria, Antiochus Epiphanes, ordered the Jews, on pain of death, to destroy their Scriptures and worship the Greek gods ... Another example is the Roman emperor Diocletian's order to have Christianity outlawed, its leaders killed, and their Bibles burned."[2] There have been many other attempts to destroy the Bible since its inception, but as Matthews writes, "The Bible has not only been preserved but translated into over two thousand languages (both ancient and modern)."[3]

I believe that because of all these translations, the Bible has been read by more people throughout the world than any other book in history. No other book could have survived all those times when unbelievers, including many people in powerful positions, tried to destroy it. The exact wording of the Bible has also survived. The scribes were meticulous in copying the Bible to scrolls, and as Matthews says, "The discovery of the Dead Sea Scrolls in 1947 confirmed that we still have the same Old Testament as they did at

Jesus's day. The survival of thousands of New Testament manuscripts confirms that the New Testament writings were also providentially preserved."[14]

The Bible was written over a period of 1,500 to 1,600 years and, by my count, by at least thirty-two known authors, along with some unknown authors, most of whom were from different times, some even centuries apart. Despite this, there are no contradictions in the Bible, which is united by a common theme—man's creation, fall, and redemption—that extends from the first book, Genesis, to the last, Revelation.

The Bible covers many people, places, and events of the Israelites, from the creation of the world all the way through the lives of Jesus, the disciples, and the apostle Paul. Even though it is impossible for the Bible to include the total history of the Israelites, it is thorough and precise in presenting everything necessary to convey God's entire plan for man. The thousands of people, places, and events portrayed in the Bible provide a complex, interwoven scenario while maintaining the common theme without a single contradiction. The pieces all fit together as perfectly as a jigsaw puzzle to convey God's plan.

The various authors, from different locations and times, could not possibly have fabricated the thousands of people, their family lineages, their intricate relationships, and all the events in the Bible in such a harmonious way. Matthew 1:1–17 gives the lineage of Jesus from Abraham to Joseph, His earthly father, and Luke 3:23–38 gives the lineage from Adam to Jesus through Mary, Jesus's mother. It is amazing that not a single father's name is left out in either of the lineages for all those generations.

There is an astounding degree of harmony among the four Gospels—Matthew, Mark, Luke, and John—as they relate the events in the life, death, and resurrection of Jesus Christ. Four different people wrote four separate accounts of the life and times of Jesus, though only Matthew and John were disciples of Jesus. Although Mark and Luke were not eyewitnesses to these events, they had access to eyewitnesses. Peter was a disciple of Jesus, and Mark's

Gospel seems to rely heavily on Peter's accounts. Peter himself wrote two books in the New Testament. Luke was a physician and therefore was meticulous and precise in his writings. He was a companion of the apostle Paul for some time and wrote his account shortly after the crucifixion of Jesus, which lends credibility to his writings. Although the gospels of Matthew, Mark, Luke, and John differ in their content, with each book containing events unique to that narrative, their versions of events included in multiple gospels are amazingly consistent. As you would expect from four different writers, there are minor variations in the details, but the variations are so minuscule that there is no doubt they are describing the same things.

The common theme throughout the Bible, which contains no contradictions despite being written by at least thirty-two different people, must be one of the most compelling arguments for its truth and accuracy. I firmly believe that the existence of a common theme wouldn't have been possible without supernatural guidance to the writers themselves.

The Bible doesn't try to hide anything either, which suggests that its authors were being completely honest. It includes both good and bad details about the lives of biblical characters such as David, Paul, and others. I give more credibility to a religion that addresses both the good and the bad of the people and events involved.

Nine

Biblical Coincidences?

The scriptures are filled with events that I maintain could not be the result of mere coincidences. In this chapter, I describe some examples.

Peter's Denials and Reaffirmations

During my tour of the Holy Land, we visited a site on the north side of the Sea of Galilee, between Magdala and Capernaum, called Peter's Primacy. This is where Jesus appeared to His disciples the third time after His resurrection. Peter and others had been fishing all night and had caught nothing. As they brought their boat closer to shore, Jesus told them to cast their nets on the other side of the boat. The Bible says that the nets became filled with 153 fish, a number that illustrates the preciseness of the Bible.

Later, standing by a fire of coals, as described in John 21:9–17, Jesus had cooked breakfast for Peter and the other fishermen. Jesus asked Peter three times if he loved Him, and each time Peter said, "Yes." Days earlier, as described in John 18:15–27, when Jesus was arrested just outside the house of Caiaphas, the high priest, on the night before His crucifixion, Peter was warming beside a fire of coals. He denied knowing Jesus three times, as Jesus had predicted in Matthew 26:34.

Many Bible scholars including Phil Crone, my Bible study teacher, suggest the scripture is showing a connection between the two scenes. Both scenes involve a fire of coals, and these are the only two times in the Bible when a fire of coals is mentioned. Also, Peter's three denials of Jesus in one scene and his three affirmations of love for Jesus in the other scene surely point to a connection rather than coincidence. I also think this suggests that Jesus gives us an opportunity to make amends for every mistake we make.

The Sacrificing of Isaac Foretells of the Crucifixion

God describes events in the Bible that foretold things that would happen later. Genesis 22 gives the account of God testing Abraham by telling him to sacrifice his son Isaac. I believe it was not by coincidence that the story of Abraham and Isaac closely parallels the events of Jesus Christ's crucifixion. God used the sacrifice of Isaac to foretell that Jesus is the Lamb of God who would willingly give His life for our sins.

- God told Abraham to offer his son Isaac as a sacrifice: "Take now thy son, thine only son Isaac, whom thou lovest, and get thee into the land of Moriah; and offer him there for a burnt offering upon one of the mountains which I will tell thee of" (Genesis 22:2). Hundreds of years later, that mountain became the Temple Mount in Jerusalem, where God's only Son Jesus was crucified.
- Isaac was about thirty-seven years old and could have overpowered his father, Abraham, who was more than a hundred years old. However, Isaac went willingly, just as Jesus willingly gave his life on the cross for our sins.
- "And Abraham took the wood of the burnt offering, and laid it upon Isaac his son" (Genesis 22:6). Similarly, the wooden cross was placed on Jesus's back for Him to carry to Calvary for His crucifixion.
- "And Abraham built an altar there, and laid the wood in order, and bound Isaac his son, and laid him on the altar

upon the wood" (Genesis 22:9). Similarly, Jesus was nailed to the wooden cross as a sacrifice for our sins.

• After Abraham agreed to carry out God's command, God told him to sacrifice a lamb instead. This lamb represents Jesus Christ, who would be sacrificed for our sins. Hundreds of years later, when John the Baptist was baptizing people in the Jordan River, he called Jesus the lamb of God. This was years before Jesus was sacrificed on the cross for our sins. The lambs that the Jews always sacrificed each year during Passover represented Jesus Christ.

The story of Abraham and Isaac is a perfect picture of God willing to sacrifice his only Son Jesus for our sins. The Bible is full of pictures like this, some of which are discussed in chapter 10. I believe these pictures were not coincidences and were preordained by God.

The Dreams of Nebuchadnezzar and Daniel

The book of Daniel gives accounts of two different dreams by two different people, King Nebuchadnezzar of Babylon and Daniel the prophet. The dreams describe the same scenario in different ways but with the same meaning. The interpretations of the dreams represent, relative to that time, the current and future powerful kingdoms of the world, which most of us studied in world history or Bible study classes.

Nebuchadnezzar's Dream

The second chapter of Daniel gives the account of a dream by King Nebuchadnezzar that was interpreted by Daniel. It's amazing that Nebuchadnezzar didn't tell Daniel what he had dreamed beforehand. The dream was of an image of a person with different sections of the body, from head to toe, made of different metals that represented the present and future kingdoms of the world. Daniel describes the image in Nebuchadnezzar's dream:

This image's head was of fine gold, his breast and his arms of silver, his belly and his thighs of brass. His legs of iron, his feet part of iron and part of clay. Thou sawest till that a stone was cut out without hands, which smote the image upon his feet that were of iron and clay, and brake them to pieces. Then was the iron, the clay, the brass, the silver, and the gold, broken to pieces together, and became like the chaff of the summer threshing floors; and the wind carried them away, that no place was found for them: and the stone that smote the image became a great mountain, and filled the whole earth. (Daniel 2:32–35)

The head of gold represents Babylon, which was the current ruling kingdom; the chest and arms of silver represent Medio-Persia; the belly and thigh of bronze represent Greece; the legs of iron represent the Roman Empire; and the feet consisting of iron and clay represent the future end-time powers. The stone that smote the image represents the Messiah, Jesus Christ. The stone crushing the image represents God setting up His kingdom through Jesus Christ, who will crush and rule all nations in the last days.

Daniel's Dream

Chapter 7, paraphrased here, describes Daniel's dream, in which beasts represent the same kingdoms from King Nebuchadnezzar's dream:

The first beast was like a lion with the wings of an eagle. The second beast was like a bear being raised up on one side. The third beast was like a leopard with four wings and four heads. The fourth beast had huge iron teeth along with ten horns. Another little horn rose up among the ten horns. It spoke bombastic words and prevailed against his enemies for a time. Then the Ancient of days slew the little horn and took away the dominion of the other beasts. Then one like the Son of man came with the clouds of heaven. Unto Him was given glory, a kingdom, and an everlasting dominion over all people, nations, and languages that would not pass away, and His kingdom would never be destroyed. All the people, nations, and languages would serve Him eternally.

The first beast, like a lion with the wings of an eagle, represents Babylon. I don't think it is a coincidence that Babylon's national symbol was a winged lion in the days of Nebuchadnezzar.

The second beast, like a bear, represents Medio-Persia, and the fact that the creature is raised up on one side represents the dominance the Persians would have over the Medes. Many years later, the Medes and Persians worked together to overthrow Babylon, but the Persians were eventually dominant over the Medes.

The third beast, like a leopard with four wings and four heads, represents Greece, which was the next world power after the Medio-Persian empire. Alexander the Great of Greece conquered the world with the speed of a leopard, and the four heads represent the division of his kingdom among his four leading generals after his death.

The fourth beast's huge iron teeth represent the powerful Roman Empire, and its ten horns represent the same kingdoms as the ten toes of Nebuchadnezzar's vision. Revelation describes the earth as being divided into ten kingdoms during the end times, under the control of the Antichrist, represented by the little horn that rose up among the ten horns.

Daniel then describes the Messiah, Jesus Christ, conquering the Antichrist and ruling all people and all nations, just as depicted by the rock in Nebuchadnezzar's dream.

The dreams of King Nebuchadnezzar and Daniel represent the same scenario—the present and future world kingdoms relative to Daniel's life, and Jesus Christ establishing His kingdom on earth to rule over all nations. The details of these corresponding descriptions could not have happened by coincidence. Both were visions from God that prophesied the future.

Jesus's Reading of Isaiah 61

The prophet Isaiah prophesied about a Messiah in the following first two verses of chapter 61 of the book of Isaiah in the eighth century BC:

> The Spirit of the Lord God is upon me, because the Lord hath anointed me to preach good tidings unto the meek; he hath sent me to bind up the brokenhearted, to proclaim liberty to the captives, and the opening of the prison to them that are bound; To proclaim the acceptable year of the Lord, and the day of vengeance of our God; to comfort all that mourn. (Isaiah 61:1–2)

During the annual Jewish feast of Yom Kippur, the Jewish rabbis read from Isaiah 61. However, they always skip these first two verses, which were kept for the Messiah to read when He came because they pertained to Him only.

Jesus went to Nazareth where He had grown up and went into the synagogue on the Sabbath during Yom Kippur and was handed the book of Isaiah to read. Jesus opened the book and read the Isaiah passage stated above but stopped short of reading "and the day of vengeance of our God; to comfort all that mourn". Jesus then closed the book and said, "This day is this scripture fulfilled in your ears." (Luke 4:16–21, author's paraphrase)

The part of the Isaiah passage that Jesus read foretold only Jesus's first coming. The last part of the passage containing "and the day of vengeance of our God" is the prophecy of Jesus's second coming during the day of vengeance, the Tribulation as described in the book of Revelation. Because this had not happened yet, Jesus stopped reading in the middle of that sentence and didn't continue with "and the day of vengeance of our God."

The first situation was the prophecy of Isaiah about Jesus, and the second was when Jesus read the words that Isaiah had prophesied about Him. These two situations, which occurred at least seven hundred years apart, go hand in hand perfectly down to the smallest detail. The precision of this fulfillment of Isaiah 61:1–2 by Jesus, in which He stops reading in the middle of a scripture passage, blows my mind. The prophecy of Isaiah and the actions of Jesus corroborate each other so perfectly that we must absolutely dismiss this as coincidence.

Hebrew Word Meanings

The Hebrew names in the Bible of certain people and places often have deep meanings. The following are four examples.

> *Bethlehem* means "house of bread." Bethlehem was the town in Israel where Jesus was born. Jesus said to His disciples, "I am the bread of life: he that cometh to me shall never hunger; and he that believeth on me shall never thirst" (John 6:35). As Jesus and His disciples were having the Lord's Supper, Matthew 26:26 says, "Jesus took bread, and blessed it, and brake it, and gave it to the disciples, and said, 'Take, eat, this is my body.'" So there must have been divine guidance given to whoever named Bethlehem, where Jesus, "the bread of life," was to be born later.

> *Jesus* is derived from *Yeshua*, which means "salvation" or "savior" in Hebrew. The Lord appeared to Joseph in a dream, telling him that Mary would conceive a child and they would name him Jesus. "And she shall bring forth a son, and thou shalt call his name *Jesus*; for he shall save his people from their sins" (Matthew 1:21). It is not a coincidence that Jesus was given this name, because He is our Savior if we believe in Him and put our trust in Him.

> *Malachi*, a name that means "my messenger," was the prophet who wrote the last book of the Old Testament, in

which he foretold a messenger to come: "Behold, I will send my messenger, and he shall prepare the way before me" (Malachi 3:1). This messenger was John the Baptist, who came before Jesus and told of his cousin, Jesus the Messiah, who would later appear. The prophet Malachi's name must have resulted from divine guidance, not coincidence.

➤ *Job* comes from the Hebrew name that means "person who is afflicted". The book of Job depicts a biblical character that was afflicted, victimized, and tortured by Satan through the loss of all his children, the loss of his vast amount of property, and physical suffering and agony. Thus the name given to Job certainly was prophetic and the result of divine intervention.

The meanings of these names were not coincidental, but rather the result of God's divine guidance, for only He can see the end from the beginning.

The next chapter, on the Jewish feasts, also logically fits into this discussion. However, because of their importance, they deserve a chapter of their own. As you will see in chapter 10, the events of the feasts amazingly parallel the life, death, and resurrection of Christ. The picture is so perfect that I believe we can rule out coincidence. The 100 percent fulfillment of the prophecies mentioned in chapter 13, concerning people, places and events of the Bible, and the 100 percent fulfillment of the prophecies mentioned in chapter 18, concerning Jesus's first coming, were not coincidental and could have been included here also.

Ten

Jewish Feasts Point to
Jesus as the Messiah

Don't let the title of this chapter mislead you into thinking that I support Judaism over Christianity. It is my contention that even though the Jews faithfully celebrate the Jewish feasts, most don't comprehend—or are just not willing to admit—how these feasts point to Jesus Christ as the Messiah. In this chapter, I show how these feasts lend great credibility to Jesus and the Bible.

In Leviticus 23, the Lord describes His seven feasts, or *festivals* as they are also called. Even though they are God's feasts, we will refer to them as Jewish feasts. God told Moses to direct the Israelites to observe His seven feasts at specific times every year. They are holy days in the Jewish religion. Most people, including many Christians, know little about these seven Jewish feasts, even though they are described in Leviticus and referred to throughout the Bible. Many Christians believe the Jewish feasts pertain only to Jews and thus tend to ignore them.

Regardless of whether you participate in the observance of these feasts, I am convinced that to really understand the Bible, one must be acquainted with many of the Old Testament Jewish traditions and customs. That is particularly true for understanding the meaning and implications of the Jewish feasts.

When I was searching for evidence supporting the Bible, I knew little of these feasts. I had heard of Passover and Pentecost, though I didn't know much about them, but study has revealed to me the significance of these feasts in God's overall plan for man. Phil Crone, my Sunday school and Bible study teacher for many years, is an Old Testament scholar and taught me many of the things I discuss in this chapter.

There are other good sources, but I chose to use quotes from *The Seven Festivals of the Messiah,* by Edward Chumney to provide the foundation—professional expertise—for this discussion. *The Seven Festivals of the Messiah,* by Edward Chumney, includes an in-depth look at each of the seven festivals, and I appreciate the author's willingness to let me quote him extensively in this chapter. It would have been difficult to write this chapter without Chumney's book and the knowledge imparted to me by Phil Crone.

Certain English names in various quotes by Chumney are followed by the corresponding Hebrew name in parenthesis and sometimes brackets. *Yeshua* is the Hebrew word for Jesus, and many Messianic Jews use *G-d* for God and *L-rd* for Lord in written text.

God mentions in Leviticus 23:2, "the feasts of the Lord, which you shall proclaim to be holy convocations." Chumney says, "The Hebrew term translated as 'convocation' in Leviticus (Vayikra) 23:2, 4 is 'miqra' which means 'a rehearsal.'"[1] The Lord is telling us that the seven Jewish feasts are rehearsals of things to come, foreshadowing great biblical events. Chumney continues: "The festivals are blueprints through which G-d revealed His overall plan of redemption for both man and the earth following the fall of man in the Garden of Eden (Gan Eden) as well as the role that the Messiah (Yeshua) would play in that redemption."[2]

The first four festivals are celebrated in the spring and depict the events of Jesus Christ's first coming. The last three are celebrated in the fall and foreshadow the events of Christ's future second coming during the last days. The interval between the spring and fall festivals represents the church age. The intricacies and accurateness of just the first three feasts in depicting the death, burial, and resurrection of Jesus Christ are amazing—irrefutable evidence for the Bible.

I restrict my discussion to a few basic highlights of the first two feasts as examples, but Chumney's book is available for a more detailed discussion and explanation of all seven feasts.

The First Festival: The Feast of Passover

The Feast of Passover is a picture of the death of Jesus Christ. Chumney says, "During Passover (Pesach), the head of each household was to take a lamb of the first year on the tenth day of the first month known as Nisan and set it aside until the fourteenth day (Exodus [Shemot] 12:3–6). In the evening of the fourteenth day, at exactly 3:00 p.m., the lamb was to be killed (Exodus [Shemot] 12:6)."[3]

The Israelites were to observe the lamb for four days to make sure it was indeed without spot or blemish, so that it could be sacrificed for Passover on Nisan 14. That night, which was the next day since the Jewish day ran from six o'clock one evening to six o'clock the next evening, they were to eat the lamb at Passover. In Leviticus 23, God tells the Israelites they must celebrate forever the Feast of Passover each year from the time of their exodus from Egypt, which was the first Passover.

In the year AD 33, the Jews observed Passover just as they had always done. On the tenth day of Nisan, the same day they carried the male lamb into the Temple in Jerusalem to be observed for four days, Jesus entered the Temple. There He was questioned for four days by the Pharisees and Sadducees, who were trying to find fault in Him. But just as the male lamb was without blemish, the people could find no fault in Jesus. Chumney writes:

> On the fourteenth of Nissan, at the third hour of the day (9:00 a.m.), the high priest (Cohen HaGadol) took the lamb and ascended the altar so he could tie the lamb in place on the altar. At the same time on that day Yeshua was tied to the tree on Mount

Moriah (Mark 15:25). At the time of the evening
sacrifice (3:00 p.m.) for Passover (Exodus [Shemot]
12:6) the high priest (Cohen HaGadol) ascended
the altar, cut the throat of the lamb with a knife,
and said the words 'It is finished' ... At the same
time, Yeshua died saying these exact words in John
(Yochanan) 19:30. Yeshua died at exactly 3:00 p.m.
(Matthew [Mattityahu] 27:45–46, 50).[4]

As you can see, Jesus fulfilled the meaning of the Passover
ritual that was performed each year. John 1:29 says, "The next day
John seeth Jesus coming unto him, and saith, Behold the Lamb of
God, which taketh away the sin of the world." Here, John the Baptist
referred to Christ as the sacrificial lamb for our sins, even though
Jesus would not be crucified until years later. John's foresight had to
have been received from God.

It is important for us to keep in mind that Passover was
celebrated for more than a thousand years before Jesus was born, and
continued until AD 70 when the Temple was destroyed. If Jesus were
an ordinary person, He could not have made all the events happen
such that they would mirror exactly the events of the sacrificial
Passover lamb. All this had to have been preordained by God from
the beginning.

The Second Festival: The Feast of Unleavened Bread

The Feast of Unleavened Bread is a picture of the burial of Jesus. The
day after Passover begins (fifteenth day of Nisan), the Passover meal,
or *Seder*, is observed in which the sacrificial lamb is eaten. Chumney
writes, "The lamb was roasted upright on a pomegranate stick. This
pomegranate stick is representative of the tree upon which Yeshua
died. The lamb was to be gutted, and its intestines were to be removed
and put over its head. Thus, the lamb is referred to as the 'crowned
sacrifice.' This is a picture of Yeshua in (Psalm [Tehillim] 22:13–18)."[5]

In biblical times, pomegranate represented royalty, and Jesus
Christ was royalty. The "crowned sacrifice" Chumney mentions

was symbolic of the crown of thorns placed on Jesus's head. And remember, this ritual was performed each year for more than a thousand years before Jesus was born. These rituals had to have been preordained by God.

Matzot is unleavened bread eaten by the Jews during Passover, because leaven represents sin in the Bible. Chumney writes as follows:

> During the Passover Seder, there is a bag called the matzatosh which contains three pieces of matzot. The middle piece of matzot is removed, broken, wrapped in linen, and buried. This piece of matzah is the afikomen. During this part of the service, the afikomen was removed from sight (this represented Yeshua being buried) and it remained hidden until later in the service.[6]
>
> In the Passover Seder service, the afikomen is redeemed by the children. The children who find the buried afikomen receive a gift. This gift is known as the promise of the father.[7]

It doesn't take a rocket scientist to see the analogy of the afikomen to Jesus. The three pieces of unleavened bread in the bag represent the Holy Trinity (Father, Son, and Holy Spirit) of which the middle piece, the afikomen, represents the Son, Jesus Christ. During the Last Supper, which was a Passover Seder meal, Jesus told His disciples that the bread they ate (afikomen) represented His body.

The breaking of the matzo bread represents the death of Jesus. Just as the afikomen is wrapped in linen and hidden, Jesus was wrapped in linen and buried (hidden in the earth). Later in the Seder the children search for the hidden afikomen. Just as the child who finds the hidden afikomen is rewarded, those who find Jesus Christ will also be rewarded. Their reward will be eternal life in heaven. Wow, what a perfect picture of Christ!

The Seder meal contains many more things that point to Jesus as the Christ. Although the third (FirstFruits) and fourth (Pentecost) feasts are not discussed here, they foreshadowed biblical events just as precisely. *The Seven Festivals of the Messiah* covers those in detail and with great explanation.

It is not by coincidence that these feasts were perfect in their rehearsal of the events associated with Jesus Christ's first coming. This shows that the Bible is truly the inspired Word of God, for no one else could have known that Jesus would be born a thousand years later as the prophetic counterpart represented by the first two feasts.

The last three feasts predict events in the future during the last days. Since the prophetic counterparts to the first four feasts have already been fulfilled in detail, we should expect the prophetic counterparts to the last three to be fulfilled just as precisely. Anyone interested in end-time prophecy can read about the last three feasts in *The Seven Festivals of the Messiah.*

Eleven

Health Instructions from God to the Israelites

The Bible describes safe practices given by God to the Israelites for maintaining health and hygiene. This was during the time of Moses, more than 3,500 years ago—or about 1,500 years before Jesus was born. Germs were not discovered by man until the nineteenth century, but God knew about them because He is the creator of all things. Without telling the Israelites of the existence of germs, He instructed them in how to protect themselves from them.

A few Old Testament scriptures are cited in this chapter to illustrate these God-given health instructions. These scriptures were instructions from God to Moses to give to the Israelites to help them remain healthy and free from disease. In "Scientific Foreknowledge and Medical Acumen of the Bible," Kyle Butt writes as follows:

> Moses penned the most advanced, flawless medical prescriptions that had ever been recorded. Furthermore, every statement that pertained to the health and medical well-being of the Israelite nation recorded by Moses could theoretically still be implemented and be completely in accord with

every fact modern medicine has learned in regard to germ spreading, epidemic disease control, communal sanitation, and a host of other medical and scientific discoveries.[1]

Keep the Sabbath Holy

In Exodus 20:8–10, God instructs the people to rest on the Sabbath: "Remember the sabbath day, to keep it holy. Six days shalt thou labour, and do all thy work: But the seventh day is the sabbath of the Lord thy God: in it thou shalt not do any work." First, God told the people to set aside the Sabbath to worship Him. Second, He gave them good medical advice about obtaining rest. God knew that people need a day of rest each week to replenish their bodies and give them physical strength as well as spiritual strength.

Optimal Time for Circumcision

One of the most intriguing medical instructions God gave the Israelites is found in Genesis 17:12: "And he that is eight days old shall be circumcised among you." Leviticus 12:3 gives this same instruction. In "Biblical Accuracy and Circumcision on the 8th Day," Bert Thompson writes, "On the eighth day, the amount of prothrombin present actually is elevated above one hundred percent of normal—and is the only day in the male's life in which this will be the case under normal conditions. If surgery is to be performed, day eight is the perfect day to do it. Vitamin K and prothrombin levels are at their peak."[2] Prothrombin and vitamin K are two main factors in blood clotting. Only God would have known about this chemistry that produced the optimal time for circumcision of male babies that would result in less bleeding.

Bathe in Running Water

Leviticus 15:13 says, "And when he that hath an issue is cleansed of his issue; then he shall number to himself seven days for his cleansing, and wash his clothes, and bathe his flesh in running water, and shall be clean." God knew that to completely rid himself of germs from an infectious sore, a person would need to bathe in running water so that the germs would be washed from his body. Washing in a pan of water would not remove the germs, for the germs would remain in the water and not be washed away. These germs might then be reapplied to the flesh during subsequent swipes of a bath cloth.

Proper Disposal of Refuse

Deuteronomy 23:13 says, "And thou shalt have a paddle upon thy weapon; and it shall be, when thou wilt ease thyself abroad, thou shalt dig therewith, and shalt turn back and cover that which cometh from thee." In this verse, God instructed the Israelites about how to prevent disease caused by refuse that could become germ-filled and infectious. They were to go outside the camp to relieve themselves and then to cover the refuse with dirt using an implement.

Containment of Leprosy

In chapter 13 of Leviticus, God gave the priests advice about how to detect leprosy from sores such as boils, risings, scabs, and so on. If leprosy was confirmed, they were to burn the person's garments. Leviticus 13:46 says, "All the days wherein the plague shall be in him he shall be defiled; he is unclean: he shall dwell alone; without the camp shall his habitation be." Anyone infected with leprosy would be infectious and would need to be quarantined to prevent spreading leprosy to others in the camp. Remember, however, germs were unknown until the nineteenth century. In Leviticus 14:33–53, God even tells the people how to cleanse their houses that are infected with these germs.

Running Issues from Body Flesh

Leviticus 15:2 says, "Speak unto the children of Israel, and say unto them, When any man hath a running issue out of his flesh, because of his issue he is unclean." God says that a person is unclean if he has unclean fluids coming from his body, since they would probably contain infectious germs. This could be puss from sores, infected blood, and so on. People should not come in contact with an unclean person during this time because they might also become infected.

Eating Certain Dead Beasts Forbidden

Leviticus 22:8 says, "That which dieth of itself, or is torn with beasts, he shall not eat to defile himself therewith; I am the Lord." If an animal died by itself, it may have succumbed to disease and thus should not be eaten. Similarly, if a dead carcass had been torn by beasts, it may have been infected by the animal that killed it. In either case, the dead animal should not be eaten.

Clean and Unclean Animals

God instructs the Israelites about clean and unclean animals in Leviticus 11:10: "And all that have not fins and scales in the seas, and in the rivers, of all that move in the waters, and of any living thing which is in the waters, they shall be an abomination unto you." Scavengers eat things on the bottoms of seas, rivers, or lakes, such as the refuse of other living things or dead carcasses that have settled to the bottom, and all these would be unhealthy.

Leviticus 11:13–19 lists various types of fowl that are not clean and should not be eaten, including vultures, ravens, hawks, owls, eagles, bats, and so on. These birds of prey eat things that are dead, many of which are infected with germs.

The first five books of the Old Testament include additional health instructions given by God to help protect the Israelites. God had to have been the source of this advanced information, and without it, the Israelites would probably have been wiped out by disease during their forty-year journey through the wilderness on their way to the Promised Land.

Part Four

Evidence for Accuracy
of the Bible

Twelve

Real People, Places, and Events Mentioned in the Bible

This chapter discusses archeology that supports the truth and accuracy of the Bible. I first share a few things about a tour of the Holy Land that were inspirational and provided biblical verification to me, followed by a small sample of archeological evidence discussed by other writers.

Holy Land Tour Provided Visual Biblical Verification

Seeing things in person that I had read about in biblical accounts was eye opening and inspiring. If you ever have the opportunity, please visit the Holy Land in Israel. It will make the Bible really come to life for you as you read the biblical accounts of Jesus, His disciples, the Old Testament patriarchs, and places and events discussed in the Bible. As we visited each site, we held a short Bible study and read verses associated with that site, which made the Bible seem alive to me. In the next few paragraphs, you'll read about places that were inspirational to me.

Most places mentioned in the Bible have been identified as real places. On my tour of the Holy Land, I visited Caesarea, Nazareth, Cana, the Sea of Galilee, Capernaum, Caesarea Philippi, Megiddo,

Mount Carmel, Jerusalem, Bethlehem, Qumran, the Mount of Olives, and the Garden of Gethsemane, among other places. I can attest that these places are real, for I have seen them in person. Other places once thought to exist only in fables, such as Sodom, Gomorrah, and Babylon, have also been found.

Brook Kishon

First Kings 18:40 says, "And Elijah said unto them, 'Take the prophets of Baal; let not one of them escape.' And they took them: and Elijah brought them down to the brook Kishon, and slew them there." Two thousand years later, the tiny Kishon brook can be seen at the base of Mount Carmel. After we drove down from Mount Carmel to its base, we passed over this little brook. It was intriguing to see something so small and seemingly insignificant mentioned in the Bible. The accuracy of such fine details in the Bible adds tremendously to the evidence for its truth.

Sea of Galilee

According to the Bible, the area around the Sea of Galilee is where Jesus did most of His preaching, and I will never forget my first glimpse of it. Our tour bus topped a hill and there it was, the Sea of Galilee that I had read about so many times in the Bible. What an awesome sight to behold!

On the second night of our tour, we stayed in a motel beside the Sea of Galilee. My room was on the fifth floor, and I could look out my window over the Sea of Galilee. The next morning, I awoke early and saw the beautiful sunrise over the water. I cannot describe the awed feeling I had, knowing that this area was the scene of much of the Gospels' accounts of Jesus and His disciples.

Our group rode on a fishing boat that was constructed supposedly like fishing boats in Jesus's day. Some men depicted fishermen casting their fishing nets as Peter and the other disciples had done. The experience was so inspiring that our large group spontaneously sang gospel songs.

Garden of Gethsemane

On the Mount of Olives in Jerusalem is the Garden of Gethsemane, which contains olive trees so old that some of them were likely there during Jesus's time. Jesus loved the Garden of Gethsemane and spent much time there. He spent His last night praying there as He awaited His arrest by Roman soldiers, which led up to His crucifixion.

Our group walked through the Garden and among the old olive trees. We had Bible study and read in Mark 14:32, "And they came to a place which was named Gethsemane: and he saith to his disciples, 'Sit ye here, while I shall pray.'" It was so humbling to be there in the Garden of Gethsemane that Jesus had loved so much and where He had prayed in agony as He awaited His arrest.

Golgotha

Another awe-inspiring place was Golgotha, the hill in Jerusalem on which Jesus and two thieves were crucified. Another name for Jesus's crucifixion site is Calvary. Golgotha is called the "place of a skull" in the Bible, because the side of the hill carries the impression of a skull, which is still there to this day. Mark 15:22 says, "And they bring him unto the place Golgotha, which is, being interpreted, The place of a skull." It is intriguing to see such fine biblical details verified by sight!

Garden Tomb

In close proximity to Golgotha is the Garden Tomb, where many people believe Jesus was buried. Most of our group members wept as they entered the tomb where I believe Jesus once lay. I touched a small model of the large heavy round stone that sealed the tomb when Jesus was buried there, and I stood in the depression (track) where the stone was rolled to seal the tomb.

But unlike everyone else who has ever been buried, Jesus was not there! He arose from the dead and is in heaven at the right hand of God the Father. Afterward, our group had an emotional communion service in a beautiful garden area just outside the tomb.

Bethlehem and Shepherd Fields

We visited a hill overlooking the shepherds' fields and the town of Bethlehem. Bethlehem is now controlled by Arabs, so we could not go into the city. Jesus was born there two thousand years ago, and it was inspiring just to glimpse it in the distance.

The shepherd fields were the same fields where the shepherds were tending their flocks on the night when Jesus was born. The shepherds saw angels praising God and saying, "Glory to God in the Highest, and on earth peace, good will toward men" as we read in Luke 2:14. We saw shepherds still tending their sheep in those same fields.

Biblical Temple Mount

Our group toured the site of the original Temple Mount in Jerusalem. The Romans destroyed the Temple in AD 70, but the Western Wall, a Jewish holy site, remains to this day. Visitors pray there, writing prayer requests on small pieces of paper and placing them in the cracks between the rocks of the wall. I placed one there myself.

Our group walked on the southern steps of the Temple Mount that remain to this day. These were the original steps the Jews used to enter the Temple to worship and give sacrifices during Jesus's time. It was inspiring to know that we walked on the same steps that Jesus walked many times as He entered and left the Temple.

Jordan River

The Jordan River connects the Sea of Galilee in northern Israel with the Dead Sea, and it was the site of many biblical events. The Israelites crossed the Jordan as they entered the land given to them by God. John the Baptist often preached at the Jordan, and he baptized many people there, including Jesus.

When we visited the Jordan River, several members of our group were baptized there by our pastor. I was one of them, and even though I had been baptized years earlier, I consider it to be my true baptism into Christianity. What an unbelievable privilege to be baptized in the same river where Jesus was baptized by John the Baptist.

Capernaum

We saw the archeological remains of the town of Capernaum, which is just north of the Sea of Galilee. Capernaum, mentioned many times in the Gospels, is where Jesus lived and did much of His preaching. The base of the synagogue where Jesus preached can still be seen today, under the base of another synagogue that was later built on top of it. There is also evidence that one of the houses located a few yards from the synagogue belonged to the disciple Peter.

Mount of Olives

The Mount of Olives, on the eastern side of the Old City of Jerusalem, is part of Jerusalem today. The Old City existed during the time of Jesus. The Mount of Olives got its name because of the many olive trees that grew there.

We spent the last two nights of our tour at a motel in Jerusalem, and I could see the Mount of Olives from my window. I got my Bible out and read Mark 16:19, about Jesus's ascension into heaven from the Mount of Olives after His resurrection: "So then after the Lord had spoken unto them, he was received up into heaven, and sat on the right hand of God." The experience of reading about this event that happened two thousand years ago and seeing the place from my window was beyond description.

Qumran and the Dead Sea Scrolls

Probably the most significant of all archeological finds that support the Bible and Christianity are the Dead Sea Scrolls, found in 1947 by a Bedouin shepherd boy at Qumran, near the Dead Sea in Israel. Searching for a lost sheep, the boy found the scrolls inside jars within caves on the side of a mountain. The scrolls had been placed there sometime between roughly 200 BC and AD 70.

On our tour we saw these caves, along with the excavated rooms where scribes had meticulously copied Hebrew scriptures to those scrolls. The scribes had placed the scrolls in the jars inside the caves to preserve them, because they were facing Roman persecution and knew that the scrolls would be destroyed. I believe this is another divine intervention to allow God's Word to be preserved and then later rediscovered.

All the books of the Old Testament except Esther are included in these scrolls. The Dead Sea Scroll version of the book of Isaiah matches exactly the King James Version that we have today. Isaiah wrote his book sometime in the eighth century BC, and it was copied to a scroll between 200 and 100 BC. This shows that the book of Isaiah was not written after the fact, as many agnostics and atheists contend. This fact is significant because Isaiah made so many prophecies about a coming Messiah that were fulfilled more than seven hundred years later by Jesus. All the other books of the King James Bible also match the Dead Sea Scrolls' versions.

Parts of the New Testament have also been found in the scrolls. This fact verifies that the New Testament is accurate in the Gospels' accounts of Jesus, since they were written soon after the life of Jesus. Little time elapsed between Jesus's death and the writing of the Gospels—further evidence of the reliability of the Bible.

Other Archeological Evidence

Dr. Randall Price says in *The Stones Cry Out,* "Archaeology has revealed the cities, palaces, temples, and houses of those who lived shoulder to shoulder with the individuals whose names appear in Scripture."[1] I highly recommend Price's book for anyone who wants an in-depth discussion about some important archeological finds that support the Bible.

Various Texts Supporting the Bible

Writings supporting the veracity of the Bible have been found on a variety of materials including papyrus, animal skins, and clay tablets, as Price says in *The Stones Cry Out*: "Such literary evidence, along with the vast array of other material remains, has built through more than a century of discovery into an impressive arsenal of evidence for the historicity and increased illumination of the biblical text."[2]

Pontius Pilate Inscription

Pontius Pilate was the Roman governor who ruled over Judea during the time of Jesus's crucifixion, and his residence was in the city of Caesarea. Skeptics and agnostics have doubted the actual existence of Pontius Pilate. However, in the old Roman theater in Caesarea, in Israel, a stone was discovered that bears an inscription of the words "Pontius Pilate." This single discovery verified the existence of a person named Pontius Pilate who sentenced Jesus to be crucified. I saw a replica of this stone just outside the Roman theater in Caesarea.

King Hezekiah's Tunnel

Second Chronicles 32 tells the story of King Hezekiah building a tunnel to preserve the Israelites' water supply from the Gihon Spring, so that Jerusalem could prevent the Assyrians from shutting off their water supply during an attack. This account is documented in *The Stones Cry Out*:

> Hezekiah managed to divert its waters by stopping the upper outlet and directing its flow to the western side of the city (see 2 Chronicles 32:2–4, 30). This was accomplished by an incredible feat of engineering that even modern engineers marvel at today. Hezekiah secretly carved through solid limestone a 1,750-foot tunnel underneath Jerusalem. This connected the Gihon Spring with

the present-day Pool of Siloam, located within the walls at the city's southwestern corner.[3]

The Hezekiah Tunnel is located exactly as stated in the Bible, and many tourists go through it daily.

Babylon

The Bible makes many references to Babylon, a town in Babylonia. Founded by King Nimrod and sometimes called "the land of Shinar," Babylonia was located in what is modern-day Iraq. Genesis 10:10 says, "And the beginning of [Nimrod's] kingdom was Babel, and Erech, and Accad, and Calneh, in the land of Shinar." Babel was the city of Babylon.

Many skeptics doubted the existence of the biblical Babylon until excavations began there in the latter part of the nineteenth century. Once the center of a huge kingdom, Babylon was where the Babylonians took many Israelites after the destruction of Jerusalem. Archeologists have found much evidence for the place as being the Babylon of the Bible.

Ebla Tablets

In "The Ebla Tablets Mystery," Amish Shah writes, "Ancient Ebla was located in Northern Syria ... In the 1970s a series of extraordinary tablets was discovered among the ruins of an ancient palace. These tablets became known as 'The Ebla Tablets' ... quite a few ancient Biblical cities are also mentioned by name in the Ebla tablets."[4]

Many agnostics and atheists believe that the cities of Sodom, Gomorrah, Admah, Zeboiim, and Zoar, which were in southern Israel near the Dead Sea and mentioned in Genesis 14, were fictional. However, Shah says, "But it turns out that the Ebla tablets refer to all five of the 'cities of the plain,' and on one tablet the cities are listed in the exact same order that we find in Genesis chapter 14."[5]

These are just a few of the many archeological finds that I contend verify the truth and accuracy of the Bible. This archeological evidence adds to our growing list of evidence that supports the Bible and thus Christianity.

Thirteen

Prophecies About People, Places, and Events Mentioned in the Bible

Prophecies are predictions about things that will happen later, and the prophets were messengers from God who told of future events. Often their prophecies would detail consequences of people not following God's Word.

The major prophets were Isaiah, Jeremiah, Ezekiel, and Daniel, and the minor prophets were Hosea, Joel, Amos, Obadiah, Jonah, Micah, Nahum, Habakkuk, Zephaniah, Haggai, Zechariah, and Malachi. The Old Testament books written by and named after these prophets contain hundreds of prophecies, and each that has been fulfilled thus far has been 100 percent accurate. With that success rate, I fully expect all prophesied future events to be fulfilled accurately as well.

In Isaiah 42:9, God tells the people that only He can foretell what is going to happen in the future and that it will all come to pass. God challenges any other so-called gods to do this: "Shew the things that are to come hereafter, that we may know that ye are gods" (Isaiah 41:23). Then God tells us that is how we should know that He is God: "For I am God, and there is none else; I am God, and there is none like me, Declaring the end from the beginning, and from ancient times the things that are not yet done, saying, My counsel shall stand, and I will do all my pleasure" (Isaiah 46:9–10).

Every prophecy in the Old Testament that was supposed to have happened by now has been fulfilled as prophesied, thus proving God is who He says He is. His Word is total, complete, and accurate. I will now discuss a few of these prophecies and their fulfillment to illustrate just how accurate they were.

Jacob's Prophecies of His Sons' Futures

Jacob was a great Bible patriarch who had twelve sons. One day in his old age, he called all his sons together and foretold to each their destiny in life, as documented in Genesis 49:1–28. All their destinies happened exactly as Jacob had predicted, which was obviously not a coincidence, since their destinies were quite varied.

Jacob prophesied this about his son Judah: "The scepter shall not depart from Judah, nor a lawgiver from between his feet, until Shiloh come; and unto him shall the gathering of the people be" (Genesis 49:10). A scepter was an ornamental staff that kings carried to represent their royalty. Jesus was among Judah's descendants and was royalty because He was the Messiah. *Shiloh* is a Hebrew term meaning "peaceful," and Jesus certainly fits that description. Wherever Jesus went and preached or taught, He always attracted a large gathering of people. So it is obvious how accurate this prophecy was.

Future King Cyrus to Release the Captive Jews

After Jerusalem was captured and destroyed by the Babylonians during the reign of King Zedekiah of Israel, the Jews were taken to Babylon as captives. In Isaiah 44:28, God says that a future king by the name of Cyrus would allow the captured Jews to be released and return home to rebuild Jerusalem: "That saith of Cyrus, He is my shepherd, and shall perform all my pleasure: even saying to Jerusalem, Thou shalt be built; and to the temple, Thy foundation shall be laid."

After the Babylonians were captured by the Persians, King Cyrus fulfilled Isaiah's prophecy. It is fascinating to note that God mentioned King Cyrus by name approximately one hundred years before he was born. Who else but God could have done that? I don't think it was just a lucky guess.

Babylon to Be Destroyed and Never to Be Rebuilt

As we learned in world history classes, Babylon was the most advanced city in all the world. No one at that time could have imagined its destruction, much less that it would never be rebuilt— no one except the prophets Isaiah and Jeremiah. Isaiah 13:19–20 and Jeremiah 51:26, 37 predict Babylon's destruction and that it will never be rebuilt. And that is exactly what happened. Isaiah 14:23 prophesies that Babylon will become a swamp: "I will also make it a possession for the bittern, and pools of water: and I will sweep it with the besom of destruction, saith the Lord of hosts."

In "From Reliable to Divine: Fulfilled Prophecy in the Old Testament," J. Varner Wallace writes, "After Cyrus conquered Babylon in 539 BC, the kingdom was destroyed and the buildings of Babylon fell into a gradual state of ruin during the next several centuries. When archaeologists excavated Babylon during the 1800s, they discovered that some parts of the city could not be uncovered because they were under a water table."[1] Wallace shows how the prophecy in Isaiah 14:23 was fulfilled perfectly. How could Isaiah have known that Babylon would become a swamp in the eighth century BC unless this knowledge was given to him by God?

Temple Stones Thrown Down

Jesus prophesied to His disciples the destruction of the Holy Temple in Jerusalem: "And Jesus said unto them, See ye not all these things? Verily I say unto you, There shall not be left here one stone upon another, that shall not be thrown down" (Matthew 24:2).

About forty years later, in AD 70, the Romans destroyed Jerusalem and set fire to the Temple. In *The Stones Cry Out*, Randall Price writes,

"This fire, it is believed, melted the gold that lined the inner walls of the buildings, causing it to flow into the cracks between the stones. This would have made it necessary for the soldiers to pull down the stones to retrieve the gold."[2] This is exactly what Jesus meant when He said, "There shall not be left here one stone upon another, that shall not be thrown down." Looks like Jesus was spot-on with His prophecy!

Jerusalem Plowed as a Field

Micah 3:12 predicts that Jerusalem will be destroyed and plowed as a field: "Therefore shall Zion for your sake be plowed as a field, and Jerusalem shall become heaps" That is exactly what happened. In "Zion Would Be 'Plowed Like a Field,'" from *About Bible Prophecy*, we read the following:

> Micah's prophecy is believed to have been delivered in about 730 BC (about 2700 years ago) ... According to a text in the Gemara—a collection of ancient Jewish writings—the Romans ran a plow over Zion on the 9th day of the Jewish month of Ab. The Gemara said that Turnus Rufus, a Roman officer, plowed the area of the Temple. This prophecy was fulfilled in literal detail.[3]

Jews Rewarded if Obedient to God

In Leviticus, God tells the Jews that if they are obedient, He will make them more powerful than their enemies: "And ye shall chase your enemies, and they shall fall before you by the sword. And five of you shall chase an hundred, and an hundred of you shall put ten thousand to flight" (26:7–8).

In 1948, Israel became a nation, and Jews from around the world started returning to their homeland. Since then, they have been more obedient to God than before their dispersion. The Arab nations have engaged in war against Israel several times since 1948, but each time the Arab nations have been soundly defeated. The total landmass of these Arab nations and their total populations are many times that of Israel, yet they still cannot defeat Israel. All this supports the prophecy in Leviticus 26:7–8.

Egypt to Be Diminished

Ezekiel prophesied that God would diminish Egypt so that it would never again rule over other nations: "It shall be the basest of the kingdoms; neither shall it exalt itself any more above the nations: for I will diminish them, that they shall no more rule over the nations" (Ezekiel 29:15).

This prophecy was given about 600 BC, and since that time Egypt has never been a world power like it had been for hundreds of years previously. Egypt fought several times with other Arab nations against Israel since 1948, but each time it lost despite being ten times larger than Israel. Chalk another one up for God!

Destruction of Capernaum, Chorazin, and Bethsaida, Never to Be Rebuilt

Jesus prophesied future destruction for three cities that had turned away from God: "Woe unto thee, Chorazin! Woe unto thee, Bethsaida! ... And thou, Capernaum, which art exalted unto heaven, shall be brought down to hell" (Matthew 11:21, 23). In these verses, Jesus condemned Capernaum, Chorazin, and Bethsaida, which were prominent, thriving cities in Israel. However, Jesus knew they would later be in perpetual ruins.

In Jesus's day, Capernaum had a large population and was prosperous because of its location. I visited Capernaum, a tourist site, on my trip to the Holy Land, and it is still in ruins. Likewise, after being destroyed, Chorazin and Bethsaida have not been rebuilt even to this day.

These are only a few examples of the many prophecies that have been fulfilled exactly as predicted, and they contribute to our growing list of evidence for the Bible.

Fourteen

Accurate Prophecies Involving Biblical Time Intervals

In this chapter, I discuss three Bible prophecies regarding biblical time intervals as examples of the accuracy of God's Word. Each prophecy specifies a definite time interval between a starting event and another prophesied event that will happen later. If those prophesied time intervals are exact, they provide tremendous credibility to the accuracy of our Bible.

Daniel's Prophecy of 483 Years

One of the most amazing prophecies about Jesus was made by the prophet Daniel: "Know therefore and understand that from the going forth of the commandment to restore and to build Jerusalem unto the Messiah the Prince shall be seven weeks, and threescore and two weeks" (Daniel 9:25).

Weeks in this biblical context represents seven, because there are seven days in a week. So seven weeks plus threescore and two weeks would be sixty-nine weeks. History has shown that the time interval in Daniel's prophecy above was many years, so the sixty-nine weeks represents sixty-nine weeks of years. Such use of terms is common in Bible scripture. The sixty-nine weeks of years would then be sixty-nine multiplied by seven, or 483 years. Therefore Daniel predicted 483 years between the commandment to restore and rebuild Jerusalem and the arrival of Messiah the Prince (Jesus Christ).

Babylon had taken the Israelites as captives to Babylon about 600 BC. Later the Medes and Persians came to power and conquered Babylon: "For we were bondmen; yet our God hath not forsaken us in our bondage, but hath extended mercy unto us in the sight of the kings of Persia, to give us a reviving, to set up the house of our God, and to repair the desolations thereof, and to give us a wall in Judah and in Jerusalem" (Ezra 9:9).

In "Daniel's 70 Weeks of Years," David Reagan lists various decrees by kings to allow the Jews to return to Jerusalem and rebuild, but he proposes the following to be most likely:

> 457 B.C.—Artaxerxes, King of Persia, issued a decree to Ezra authorizing him to reinstitute the Temple services, appoint judges and magistrates, and teach the Law (Ezra 7:11–26) ... the Jews were authorized to launch a general rebuilding campaign that included the temple, the city, and the walls ... Now, using Ezra's decree as the starting point (457 B.C.), if we count forward 483 years we arrive at 27 A.D. (There is only one year between 1 B.C. and 1 A.D.) ... This is most likely the year that Jesus began His public ministry ... Further evidence that this date is correct is the fact that it would place the end of Jesus' 3½ year ministry in the spring of 31 A.D. And that happens to be the most likely year of the crucifixion.[1]

Thus we see from Reagan's analysis that the prophecy in Daniel 9:25 of 483 years was fulfilled exactly as predicted.

Abraham's Descendants to Be Afflicted for Four Hundred Years

The people of Ur, also called the Land of the Chaldeans, began to worship other gods. Abraham was a godly man, and God told him that if his people would leave Ur, He would provide another land for them. However, during all this time they were sojourners in a land that was not theirs, so they were always afflicted by other people and nations. They were sojourners until their exodus from Egypt.

Later, after Abraham had left Ur and many years had passed, God told him that he would have many descendants. Both Abraham and his wife, Sarah, were old, and they didn't think it was possible for Sarah to bear Abraham a child. So with Sarah's blessing, Abraham had a son named Ishmael by a bondwoman named Hagar so that he would have descendants.

However, as God had promised, Sarah did later bear Abraham a son, and they named him Isaac. God told Abraham, "For in Isaac shall thy seed be called" (Genesis 21:12). So God told Abraham that his descendants would be through Isaac, not Ishmael. God also told Abraham, "Know of a surety that thy seed shall be a stranger in a land that is not theirs, and shall serve them; and they shall afflict them four hundred years" (Genesis 15:13).

Isaac was born thirty years after this revelation by God. Scripture shows that there were four hundred years between the birth of Isaac and when the Israelites left Egypt and received their freedom.

"Now the sojourning of the children of Israel, who dwelt in Egypt, was four hundred and thirty years. And it came to pass at the end of the four hundred and thirty years, even the selfsame day it came to pass, that all the hosts of the Lord went out from the land of Egypt" (Exodus 12:40–41).

The four hundred and thirty years mentioned here is the total time from the revelation in Genesis 15:13 above of Abraham's seed (Isaac) until the Israelites obtained their freedom as they left Egypt. If we take the thirty years for the birth of Isaac from the total years of sojourning to the freedom of the Israelites from the Egyptians, we determine that there was exactly four hundred years for the seed of Abraham to be a stranger and afflicted in a land that was not theirs.

Thus the prophecy of Genesis 15:13 was exactly fulfilled as shown in Exodus 12:40–41.

Israelites Captive by Babylonians for Seventy Years

During the prophet Jeremiah's time, Israel had turned away from God and the people were worshipping idols—evil, wicked, and filled with perversion. God told them, "They are all of them unto me as Sodom, and the inhabitants thereof as Gomorrah" (Jeremiah 23:14). The prophet Jeremiah had repeatedly warned them of impending doom if they didn't turn to God and start living right. Finally Jeremiah gave them this amazing prophecy: "And this whole land shall be a desolation, and an astonishment; and these nations shall serve the king of Babylon seventy years" (Jeremiah 25:11).

In "Jeremiah's Seventy Years," Robert J. Morgan gives four explanations for how we arrive at seventy years as a precise fulfillment of Jeremiah's prophecy. Here are three of his explanations.

- The Assyrian Empire fell to Babylon in 609, and the Babylon Empire fell to Persia in 539. That is exactly 70 years. The Babylon Empire had a lifespan of exactly 70 years between the fall of Assyria and the rise of Persia, during which time Judah was threatened or in subjection.
- I like this theory even better. The temple of Solomon was destroyed by Babylon in 587 BC. The Second temple was completed and dedicated in 517 BC, which is exactly 70 years.
- Perhaps the best view of all is to calculate the date from the first invasion of Nebuchadnezzar in 605 B.C. to the laying of the foundation of the Second Temple in 536 B.C. That was exactly 70 years.[2]

No matter which of Morgan's calculations you use, each shows that the Babylonians held the Israelites captive for seventy years as prophesied by Jeremiah. These three examples illustrate just how exact God's Word is.

These precisely prophesied time intervals by Daniel, Moses, and Jeremiah could not have happened without the divine guidance of God. This is just more evidence to corroborate the Bible.

Fifteen

Prophecies About End Times

Both the Old Testament and New Testament contain prophecies concerning the end times. Many of these prophecies have already begun to be fulfilled, providing further evidence for the truth and accuracy of the Bible. This also shows that we are fast approaching the last days before Jesus Christ will return and rule over all the earth during the millennial kingdom. This chapter documents several of these end-time prophecies and how the events pertaining to them are beginning to take shape.

Jerusalem: An International Problem

Zechariah prophesied that as we get close to the end times, Jerusalem will be an international problem: "And in that day will I make Jerusalem a burdensome stone for all people: all that burden themselves with it shall be cut in pieces, though all the people of the earth be gathered together against it" (Zechariah 12:3).

As predicted, Jerusalem seems to be garnering much attention from the entire world. Time after time the United Nations Security Council has brought resolutions against Israel, but Israel has usually been spared because the United States votes against such resolutions.

Rarely has the United Nations scrutinized the Arab nations like they have Israel.

Just recently President Trump moved the US Embassy from Tel Aviv to Jerusalem. This caused a great uproar, both from other nations and among many Americans, thus showing just how contentious Jerusalem really is. Even though Israel is probably our greatest ally, it seems as though some members of our own government support the Palestinians over the Jews.

Temple Is Required for Sacrifices

Daniel makes the following prophecy concerning a future temple:

> And he shall confirm the covenant with many for one week: and in the midst of the week he shall cause the sacrifice and the oblation to cease, and for the overspreading of abominations he shall make it desolate, even until the consummation, and that determined shall be poured upon the desolate. (Daniel 9:27)

As explained in the previous chapter, one week in this context means seven years. This scripture tells of the Antichrist making a covenant of peace with Israel for seven years, but breaking it after three and a half years, thus causing the sacrificing to cease.

The Bible says that people will perform animal sacrifices during the millennial kingdom. A temple is required for sacrifices to take place in Israel, and obviously the temple must be constructed beforehand. The Temple Foundation in Israel has already prepared all the items necessary for the operation of the Temple that will be placed in the third Temple when it is constructed. We toured the Temple Institute in Jerusalem and saw these items that were built according to precise biblical specifications as given by God.

The Antichrist to Create a One-World Economy

John writes in Revelation of a coming Antichrist that will rule the world and try to force all people to take his mark or name in order to buy and sell:

> And he causeth all, both small and great, rich and poor, free and bond, to receive a mark in their right hand, or in their foreheads: And that no man might buy or sell, save he that had the mark, or the name of the beast, or the number of his name. (Revelation 13:16–17)

I believe this scripture implies a one-world economy during the time of the Antichrist. There are many prominent people, including in the United States, working to make this one-world economy happen.

The Antichrist to Create a One-World Government

Revelation 13:7–8 says this about the Antichrist:

> And it was given unto him to make war with the saints, and to overcome them: and power was given him over all kindreds, and tongues, and nations. And all that dwell upon the earth shall worship him, whose names are not written in the book of life of the Lamb slain from the foundation of the world.

I believe the Antichrist will be in control of all nations and all people for a time. Many nations have been advocating for globalism, which basically constitutes a one-world government and economy. Even many leaders of the United States support this political ideology. Their desire to eliminate borders and to implement socialism seems to be evidence for that.

Jesus Tells His Disciples of Things Near the End Times

Chapters 24 and 25 of Matthew contain the Olivet Discourse given by Jesus on the Mount of Olives to His disciples concerning the end times. "And as he sat upon the mount of Olives, the disciples came unto him privately, saying, Tell us, when shall these things be? and what shall be the sign of thy coming, and of the end of the world?" (Matthew 24:3). Jesus answered those questions in the following scriptures:

> Matthew 24:7: "For nation shall rise against nation, and kingdom against kingdom: and there shall be famines, and pestilences, and earthquakes, in divers places."

These things that Jesus mentioned have never been more apparent than today. Observe all the conflicts between nations and how terrorism and violent gangs have spread throughout the world. Watch television and you will see people starving around the world. Look at the increase in diseases, many of which have no known cure. Over the last few years, the number of earthquakes has been increasing at an exponential rate around the world.

> Matthew 24:11: "And many false prophets shall rise, and shall deceive many."

Observe all the false prophets who have been successful at deceiving people, sometimes founding cults. Some have even claimed to be the Messiah. What is disturbing is how many people are gullible and buy into their unrealistic ideologies and beliefs.

Many self-proclaimed psychics, with money as their objective, contend that they can give people advice about their future. Other psychics claim they can contact people's relatives who have died. There are self-proclaimed prophets who have made many predictions over the past, but most of their predictions have not come about. Compare this with all the prophecies made in the Old Testament that have so far all come about with 100 percent accuracy.

➢ Matthew 24:12: "And because iniquity shall abound, the love of many shall wax cold." Also, the apostle Peter made this prophecy: "Knowing this first, that there shall come in the last days scoffers, walking after their own lusts" (2 Peter 3:3). People are becoming more and more oblivious to the Word of God. Just look at our society today as compared with twenty-five years ago. Look at the tremendous increase in crime and the rapid decline in values and morality. At an ever-increasing rate, we have been turning away from God and instead toward our own desires and lusts. Look at the gangs and crime in our cities and how corrupt many of our leaders and politicians are.

Even though Christianity is being preached throughout the world, God is being left out of the picture. The number of Christian churches and the people who attend is steadily decreasing at an alarming rate. Our society is in a state of decline in which our morals and values have deteriorated to all-time lows.

Many atheists are pushing to take God out of everything. They have succeeded in removing prayer and Bible reading from public schools, and this has contributed much to a deterioration in morals, values, behavior, and thus achievement in the classroom. Many support abortions at any stage of pregnancy, right up to the last minute before a child is born. I am afraid that our nation will be held responsible by God for such egregious actions.

Many people are concerned only about themselves. For them, it's all about "Me!" They are out to get whatever they can, whenever they can, regardless of any negative effect on others. They have no conscience when it comes to following God's commandments.

When I was a teenager and would go out with friends at night, my parents were not afraid to leave the doors unlocked so that I would not disturb their sleep when I returned home. Can you imagine going to bed without locking your doors today? I would not get a wink of sleep, for fear that someone might enter and steal from me—or worse. My, how things have changed for the worse! I truly believe our society will continue to deteriorate until Lord Jesus returns.

➢ Matthew 24:14: "And this gospel of the kingdom shall be preached in all the world for a witness unto all nations; and then shall the end come."

Christian missionaries go to basically every part of the world spreading their message. Many evangelists, such as Franklin Graham, John Hagee, and others carry the gospel around the world. Christian television ministries such as Trinity Broadcasting Network, Christian Broadcasting Network, Daystar, and others send their Christian ministry programs to most nations around the world today by satellite.

Seas and Waves Will Roar

One fascinating prediction that Jesus told His disciples about the end times is documented in Luke 21:25. This was right after His final entry into Jerusalem and not long before His crucifixion. Luke 21:25 says, "And upon the earth distress of nations, with perplexity; the sea and the waves roaring."

There is certainly much disagreement about politics and theology around the world, often resulting in perplexing and distressing conflicts. However the last part of this prediction is particularly intriguing because of the recent increase in hurricanes, which have produced havoc in the United States and elsewhere. Just look at the destruction and loss of lives caused by high winds and flooding in coastal regions. It appears that Jesus was referring to this moment in time.

Dispersion of the Jews Followed by Their Return to Their Homeland

The dispersion of the Israelites from Israel into nations around the world was prophesied by Jesus Himself: "And they shall fall by the edge of the sword, and shall be led away captive into all nations: and Jerusalem shall be trodden down of the Gentiles, until the times of the Gentiles be fulfilled" (Luke 21:24). This is exactly what happened over the centuries, from the time of the capture of Jerusalem by the Babylonians until just recently. The Jews were indeed dispersed throughout all the nations of the world.

Jeremiah, among others, prophesied that the Jews would return to their homeland of Israel right before Christ returns: "Hear the word of the Lord, O ye nations, and declare it in the isles afar off, and say, He that scattered Israel will gather him, and keep him, as a shepherd doth his flock" (Jeremiah 31:10). Since Israel became a nation in 1948, the Jews have been returning to Israel in record numbers, thus fulfilling Jeremiah's prophecy.

Israel to Desolation Followed by Productivity

Moses warned the people that because of their disobedience to God, "Cursed shalt thou be in the city, and cursed shalt thou be in the field. Cursed shall be thy basket and thy store. Cursed shall be the fruit of thy body, and the fruit of thy land" (Deuteronomy 28:16–18). For many centuries, Israel had been a desolate and forlorn land as foretold by Moses. However, the prophet Isaiah prophesized the return of the land of Israel from desolation to productivity leading up to the last days:

> Thou shalt no more be termed Forsaken; neither shall thy land any more be termed Desolate. (Isaiah 62:4)
> He shall cause them that come of Jacob to take root: Israel shall blossom and bud, and fill the face of the world with fruit. (Isaiah 27:6)

These prophecies by Isaiah have certainly come to pass. Israel is now a prosperous and affluent nation. Israel now has bountiful fruit crops of many types and furnishes many other nations with those fruits. Israel even ships tulips to Holland. Imagine that!

Future Technology Allowing All Nations to See Two Witnesses Killed in Jerusalem

Chapter 11 of Revelation says that two witnesses will prophesy and perform miracles for 1,260 days (three and a half prophetical years) in Israel during the time of tribulation when the Antichrist's forces are in control of Jerusalem. These two witnesses will be killed, and their bodies will be left lying in the street in Jerusalem:

> And when they shall have finished their testimony, the beast that ascendeth out of the bottomless pit shall make war against them, and shall overcome them, and kill them. And their dead bodies shall lie in the street of the great city ... And they of the people and kindreds and tongues and nations shall see their dead bodies three days and an half, and shall not suffer their dead bodies to be put in graves. (Revelation 11:7–9)

I interpret the last verse as indicating that people from all nations of the world will be able to see this event. The book of Revelation was written by John, the beloved disciple of Jesus, only a few years after Jesus was crucified. Only with the development of television and the internet could this viewing be done by people around the world. Do you think that people two thousand years ago knew that visual communication like television or the internet would be available? John had to have written the book of Revelation under the divine guidance of God.

Events are beginning to take shape for the return of our Lord, as prophesied by the Old Testament prophets, which adds to the list of evidences already established for the Bible.

Sixteen

Historical Documents That Support the Bible

This chapter looks at several historical documents other than the Bible that support the teachings of Christianity and add to the growing list of evidences for the Bible.

Koran

Even though the Islam religion rejects the notion that Jesus was the Messiah, it offers some support for the Bible. The Koran, Islam's holy book, teaches that Jesus was born of the Virgin Mary, just like the Bible does, and recognizes him as a great teacher and prophet. It also recognizes the Old Testament patriarchs such as Noah, Abraham, and Moses.

Septuagint

After Alexander the Great of Greece conquered most of the known world, many people spoke Greek. The Hebrews translated the scriptures from Hebrew to Greek in a volume called the Septuagint during the third century BC, approximately three hundred years before the birth of Christ. The Septuagint thus provides further support for the Old Testament prophecies concerning Jesus. In fact, Jesus taught from the Septuagint on many occasions, quoting prophecies the prophets had made about Him.

Flavius Josephus's Writings

Flavius Josephus, born shortly after Christ's crucifixion in AD 33, was a renowned Jewish historian. Any of his accounts of Jesus's life that agree with biblical accounts lend credibility to the validity of Christianity.

William Whiston translated Josephus's two books, *The Antiquities of the Jews* and *The Wars of the Jews*, in 1737 and combined them into one volume titled *The Complete Works of Flavius Josephus*. The following passages are taken from Whiston's translation of *The Antiquities of the Jews*.

> ➤ In chapter 3 of book 18, Josephus writes as follows:
> Now there was about this time Jesus, a wise man, if it be lawful to call him a man; for he was a doer of wonderful works, a teacher of such men as receive the truth with pleasure. He drew over to him both many of the Jews and many of the Gentiles. He was [the] Christ. And when Pilate, at the suggestion of the principal men amongst us, had condemned him to the cross, those that loved him at the first did not forsake him; for he appeared to them alive again the third day; as the divine prophets had foretold these and ten thousand other wonderful things concerning him.[1]

This passage certainly supports the Gospels' accounts of Jesus. The fact that Josephus was a Jewish Pharisee and still writes this account of Jesus makes it credible, without question, because the Jews generally didn't believe that Jesus was the Messiah (Christ).

> Mark 6:14–28 tells of King Herod having John the Baptist put to death. In chapter 5 of book 18, Josephus gives the same account:

> > Herod, who feared lest the great influence John had over the people might put it into his power and inclination to raise a rebellion, (for they seemed ready to do any thing he should advise,) thought it best, by putting him to death, to prevent any mischief he might cause, and not bring himself into difficulties, by sparing a man who might make him repent of it when it would be too late. Accordingly he was sent a prisoner, out of Herod's suspicious temper, to Macherus, the castle I before mentioned, and was there put to death.[2]

> In chapter 5 of book 18, Josephus wrote of John the Baptist:

> > Now some of the Jews thought that the destruction of Herod's army came from God, and that very justly, as a punishment of what he did against John, that was called the Baptist: for Herod slew him, who was a good man, and commanded the Jews to exercise virtue, both as to righteousness towards one another, and piety towards God, and so to come to baptism;[3]

> This passage verifies the account in Mark 1:2–8 of the preaching and baptizing of the people by John the Baptist.

> In chapter 8 of book 6, Josephus tells of God selecting David to replace Saul as king of Israel after Saul had disobeyed God:

> > And when Samuel mourned for him, God bid him leave off his concern for him, and to take the holy oil, and go to Bethlehem, to Jesse the son of Obed, and to anoint such of his sons as he should show him for their future king.[4]

> God used the prophet Samuel to facilitate the selection of one of Jesse's sons to be king. None of the older sons were acceptable to God, so God had them bring in David from the shepherd's field. Josephus writes about Samuel telling David that God had selected him to be king of Israel:

So he sat down to the feast, and placed the youth under him, and Jesse also, with his other sons; after which he took oil in the presence of David, and anointed him, and whispered him in the ear, and acquainted him that God chose him to be their king.[5]

Chapter 16 of 1 Samuel gives this same account of God selecting David to be the next king.

In the scenarios documented above, Josephus's writings and the Bible agree in people, places, and events mentioned to such a high degree that it is impossible to agree with one without agreeing with the other. Since most scholars support the writings of Josephus as being accurate, we should therefore accept the validity of the Bible.

Part Five

Evidence for the
Jesus of the Bible

Seventeen

Jesus, His Disciples, and Early Christians

Few scholars dispute the fact that Jesus existed as a person during the time written about in the Gospels, since this is well documented. However, many people don't believe that Jesus was the Messiah and that He was resurrected from the grave. In this chapter and the next chapter, I attempt to provide evidence that Jesus was indeed the Messiah prophesied in the Old Testament, who was crucified and rose from the grave after three days.

Jesus had to have been the most important person ever to have lived. The Gregorian calendar is the most widely used calendar in the world and is based on Jesus's birth. It refers to dates of events as either BC or AD. Also, Christianity is the predominant religion in the world.

On His last journey to Jerusalem, Jesus told His disciples exactly what was going to happen to Him there: "Behold, we go up to Jerusalem; and the Son of man shall be betrayed unto the chief priests and unto the scribes, and they shall condemn him to death. And shall deliver him to the Gentiles to mock, and to scourge, and to crucify him: and the third day he shall rise again" (Matthew 20:18–19).

Jesus didn't run for His life when faced with impending death. His purpose on this earth was to die for our sins, and He was determined to fulfill that purpose. If Jesus hadn't known that He was sent by God the Father to fulfill that purpose, would He have *willingly* gone through a horrifying crucifixion? Jesus was beaten and scourged beyond recognition for our sins. Anyone willingly ridiculed, beaten, scourged, and crucified for a cause must surely know that cause to be true.

Before his conversion, the apostle Paul harshly persecuted Christians, hunting them down and delivering them to be killed. One day while Paul was on his way to Damascus, the resurrected Jesus appeared and asked Paul why he was persecuting the Christian people. Jesus told Paul to go to Damascus, where he would be told what he must do, and Paul willingly did just that. It took only a moment for Jesus to change Paul. After his conversion, Paul's only mission in life was to preach Christianity to as many people as possible, and he wrote several books of the New Testament. Willing to give his life for the teachings of Christianity, Paul was imprisoned and eventually beheaded.

As mentioned earlier, most scholars don't dispute that Jesus was a real person who existed in Israel during the time written about in the Gospels. They also believe that He was crucified and His body placed in a grave, as described in the Gospels. They don't dispute that His body was not in the grave on the third day, as had been foretold by Jesus Himself and other Bible prophets. However, they don't believe—or just won't admit—that Jesus was the Christ and rose from the grave. The following points suggest otherwise.

> ➤ Pilate ordered Roman guards placed at the tomb to prevent someone from stealing Jesus's body so that His followers could not claim that He was resurrected:

>> Now the next day, that followed the day of the preparation, the chief priests and Pharisees came together unto Pilate, Saying, Sir, we remember that

that deceiver said, while he was yet alive, After three days I will rise again. Command therefore that the sepulchre be made sure until the third day, lest his disciples come by night, and steal him away, and say unto the people, He is risen from the dead: so the last error shall be worse than the first. Pilate said unto them, Ye have a watch: go your way, make it as sure as ye can. So they went, and made the sepulchre sure, sealing the stone, and setting a watch. (Matthew 27:62–66)

Pilate took extraordinary precautions to guard the tomb where Jesus was buried. The stone that sealed the tomb weighed several hundred pounds. If Jesus had been an ordinary person, He could not have moved the stone by Himself. If the disciples had moved the stone, they would have made enough noise to awaken the Roman soldiers on the night watch, assuming they might have fallen sleep. But the soldiers would not have gone to sleep, for they knew they would suffer severe penalty, probably death ordered by Pilate, if they had allowed Jesus's body to be taken.

➤ I think Sam Storms's article "10 Things You Should Know about the Empty Tomb of Jesus" provides adequate confirmation that Jesus rose from the grave. Here is Storms's most compelling reason:

> If the disciples stole the body they obviously knew that Jesus didn't rise again. And if they knew the resurrection was a myth that they themselves had concocted, why did they so willingly and joyfully endure such persecution and eventual martyrdom? People don't typically die horrible deaths for something they know isn't true, unless, of course, they are certifiably insane.[1]

Eleven of the disciples, all except John, died from horrendous persecution because they would not stop ministering Christianity to the people despite death threats by the Romans.

➢ The napkin (prayer shawl or *tallit*) that had been wrapped around Jesus's head when He was buried was found apart from the burial linens and wrapped neatly in a way that proved that Jesus did it Himself. These verses imply that when John saw the wrapped napkin, he believed that Jesus had arisen: "And the napkin, that was about his head, not lying with the linen clothes, but wrapped together in a place by itself. Then went in also that other disciple, which came first to the sepulchre, and he saw, and believed" (John 20:7–8). I believe there are two explanations for why John saw and then believed.

First, every Jew had a specific way of folding his prayer shawl. Jesus's disciples, who had spent a lot of time with Him, knew how Jesus folded His prayer shawl. The disciple John observed that the napkin that had been wrapped around Jesus's head in the tomb was folded just like they had seen Jesus fold His own prayer shawl many times.

Second, if Jesus's body had been stolen, the thieves would have been in a hurry and would not have taken the time to remove the linen clothes in which Jesus's body was wrapped. Why would they have neatly folded the napkin and placed it to the side? They would have taken the body with the wrappings and left immediately to avoid being caught. This proves that Jesus's body was not stolen, as some atheists and agnostics believe. The only explanation is that Jesus arose from the grave.

➢ The disciples had thought that Jesus was the Messiah who would rule the world at that time, not later at His second coming, so after His crucifixion, they began having doubts. When they found out that Jesus's body was missing from the grave, some disciples didn't initially believe that Jesus had risen from the dead. At first, they thought the body had been stolen.

But later they willingly risked their lives to preach Christianity, and only the appearance of the resurrected Christ could have caused such a change of heart. They knew beyond the shadow of a doubt that Jesus was the Christ. More than five hundred people saw Jesus after He was resurrected. James, the half-brother of Jesus, was a skeptic but became a believer after witnessing the resurrected Jesus. He even became the head of the church in Jerusalem and wrote the book of James in the New Testament.

Matthew, John, and Peter witnessed firsthand the things they wrote about. Peter, when faced with death by crucifixion, requested that he be hanged upside down since he was unworthy of being crucified like Jesus, who had been crucified upright. John was the only disciple who didn't die from persecution, but even he was imprisoned for a time on the island of Patmos in his old age.

Another fact that lends a lot of credibility to Jesus being the Christ is that no one has ever claimed that Jesus did anything bad, wrong, or in any other way negative. In all the world, there never has been another who can lay claim to such perfection. Jesus was perfect in every way. How could that be if Jesus were not the Christ?

Eighteen

Prophecies About Jesus's First Coming

There are at least three hundred prophecies of the Messiah in the Old Testament, and those that pertain to His first coming have all been fulfilled with 100 percent accuracy. This didn't happen by chance, and I'm sure the remaining prophecies will be fulfilled just as precisely when Jesus returns to establish His kingdom on earth.

Most atheists and some agnostics say that the Old Testament was written after the fact, but that theory was squelched with the discovery of the Dead Sea Scrolls, as discussed in chapter 12.

Jesus talked about the Old Testament prophets and claimed that He was the Messiah foretold by them. On many occasions in the Gospels, He gave great credibility to them because He cited prophecies by Isaiah, Daniel, David, and others from hundreds of years earlier.

When Jesus was born, the hundreds of prophecies about a coming Messiah had already been written and could not have been changed. Jesus fulfilled every one of them down to the finest detail. Nothing was foretold about Jesus's first coming that didn't happen, and nobody else ever came close to satisfying such prophecies. Following is a small sample of the many prophecies about Jesus.

Messiah to Be Born in Bethlehem

The prophet Micah prophesied that the Messiah would be born in Bethlehem: "But thou, Beth-lehem Ephratah, though thou be little among the thousands of Judah, yet out of thee shall he come forth unto me that is to be ruler in Israel; whose goings forth have been from of old, from everlasting" (Micah 5:2).

Seven to eight hundred years later, Luke 2:1 says, "And it came to pass in those days, that there went out a decree from Caesar Augustus, that all the world should be taxed." Joseph and Mary went to the city of David, which was Bethlehem, to be accounted for and taxed because Joseph was of the lineage of King David. While they were in Bethlehem, Jesus was born of Mary, fulfilling Micah's prophecy: "And so it was, that, while they were there, the days were accomplished that she should be delivered" (Luke 2:6).

Messiah to Be Born of a Virgin

Isaiah 7:14 says that the Messiah would be born of a virgin: "Therefore the Lord himself shall give you a sign; Behold, a virgin shall conceive, and bear a son, and shall call his name Immanuel." Mary, a young virgin, was betrothed (engaged) to Joseph during the conception of Jesus. At first Joseph didn't believe that Mary had been faithful to him, because they had never had intimate relations. However, an angel appeared to Joseph and told him that Mary had conceived by the Holy Spirit and without man. After that, Joseph believed that Mary had been faithful to him and that she would be the mother of our Lord.

Lineage of the Messiah

The Old Testament foretold Jesus's lineage. Genesis 17:19 says that He would be of the seed of Isaac. Numbers 24:17 says that He would be of the seed of Jacob. Genesis 49:10 says that He would be from the tribe of Judah. Second Samuel 7:12–16 says the Messiah would be through the lineage of King David. All these prophecies were fulfilled.

Messiah to Be Preceded by a Forerunner

Malachi 3:1 says the Messiah would be preceded by a forerunner who would prepare the way before Him. This prophecy was fulfilled by John the Baptist, the cousin of Jesus who preached of the coming of a savior. Born before Jesus, John the Baptist baptized Him and proclaimed that Jesus was the Lamb of God that would take away our sins.

Prophecy of Simeon about Jesus

Simeon was a just and devout man in Jerusalem: "And it was revealed unto him by the Holy Spirit, that he should not see death, before he had seen the Lord's Christ" (Luke 2:26). As was customary by Jewish law, forty days after Jesus's birth, He was brought into the temple to be dedicated to the Lord. During this occasion, Simeon took the baby Jesus into his arms and told Mary that he had seen his Savior Jesus: "For mine eyes have seen thy salvation" (Luke 2:30). Then he prophesied that Mary's heart, along with many others, would be broken, as was later fulfilled by Jesus's crucifixion: "(Yea, a sword shall pierce through thy own soul also,) that the thoughts of many hearts may be revealed" (Luke 2:35).

Gifts of the Wise Men to the Baby Jesus

As previously discussed, the prophet Micah prophesized that the Lord Jesus would be born in Bethlehem. When Jesus was born, wise men (Magi) from the East followed the star provided by God leading them to Bethlehem, the place where Jesus was born. Matthew 2:11 says, "And when they were come into the house, they saw the young child with Mary his mother, and fell down, and worshipped him; and when they had opened their treasures, they presented unto him gifts; gold, and frankincense, and myrrh."

The three gifts to the baby Jesus were significant in that each had a prophetic meaning about Jesus's life. Due to its value, the gift of gold represented that Jesus would be royalty. Jesus is, indeed, the King of all kings. The gift of frankincense prophesied that Jesus would be deity since it was incense that was burned by the priests during worship services. Myrrh was used as an embalming oil during Jesus's time and this gift prophesied that Jesus would be sacrificed. These gifts accurately foretold the life of Jesus here on earth.

Messiah to Enter Jerusalem on a Donkey

Zechariah prophesied the arrival of King Jesus into Jerusalem: "Rejoice greatly, O daughter of Zion; shout, O daughter of Jerusalem: behold, thy King cometh unto thee: he is just, and having salvation; lowly, and riding upon an ass, and upon a colt the foal of an ass" (Zechariah 9:9). In this verse, written hundreds of years earlier, Zechariah prophesied that the Messiah would ride into Jerusalem on a colt. This prophecy was fulfilled exactly as written, as shown in Matthew 21:1–11. Days before His crucifixion, Jesus made His triumphal entry into Jerusalem on Palm Sunday riding on a young donkey.

Betrayal of Jesus

In Psalm 41:9, Jesus prophesied his own betrayal: "Yea, mine own familiar friend, in whom I trusted, which did eat of my bread, hath lifted up his heel against me." This prophecy was fulfilled in Matthew 26:46–50 when one of Jesus's disciples, Judas Iscariot, who had eaten the Passover meal (Last Supper) with Jesus, betrayed Him for thirty pieces of silver. This betrayal led to Jesus's crucifixion.

Isaiah 53 Prophesies Specific Details of Jesus's Crucixion

Chapter 53 of Isaiah foretold many specific details of the crucifixion of Jesus Christ, which would happen seven to eight hundred years later. The Romans didn't begin using crucifixion as a method of execution until hundreds of years after this prophecy was made, so how could Isaiah have known of the impending crucifixion of Jesus without divine guidance from God?

The following verses from Isaiah 53 illustrate the specific details foretold by Isaiah about Jesus's crucifixion, all of which would be fulfilled:

- Verse 3: "He is despised and rejected of men ... we esteemed him not." The Jews despised Jesus and demanded that He be crucified by the Romans. They charged Him with blasphemy because they didn't believe He was the Christ.
- Verse 5: "But he was wounded for our transgressions, he was bruised for our iniquities ... and with his stripes we are healed." Jesus willingly gave His life for our sins. He was beaten severely with whips that left stripes on His body.
- Verse 6: "The Lord hath laid on him the iniquity of us all." God sent His Son Jesus to take on Himself all our sins. The shedding of blood was required for redemption. Jesus shed His precious blood on that cross for us.
- Verse 7: "He was oppressed, and he was afflicted, yet he opened not his mouth: he is brought as a lamb to the slaughter, and as a sheep before her shearers is dumb, so he openeth not his mouth." Jesus was interrogated and beaten beyond belief, yet He didn't attempt to defend himself because He knew that His purpose was to die for our sins.
- Verse 8: "He was taken from prison and from judgment: and who shall declare his generation? for he was cut off out of the land of the living: for the transgression of my people was he stricken." The phrase "He was cut off" meant that Jesus would be killed, and He died for our sins.
- Verse 9: "And he made his grave with the wicked, and with the rich in his death; because he had done no violence, neither was any deceit in his mouth." Jesus was crucified between two thieves. Joseph, a rich man from Arimathea, asked Pilate for Jesus's body, and his request was granted.

He buried Jesus in his own new tomb. Jesus never spoke with any deceit, for He was the only perfect being to ever live on earth.

- Verse 10: "Yet it pleased the Lord to bruise him; he hath put him to grief: when thou shalt make his soul an offering for sin" Yes, Jesus died for our sins so that we might be saved, which was the plan of His Father all along.

Psalm 22 Prophesies Specific Details of Jesus's Crucifixion

Psalm 22 foretold in detail the things that Jesus would endure during His crucifixion. Like the book of Isaiah, the Psalms were written hundreds of years before Jesus was born.

- Verses 7–8: "All they that see me laugh me to scorn: they shoot out the lip, they shake their head saying, He trusted on the Lord that he would deliver him: let him deliver him, seeing he delighted in him." This passage describes exactly what happened as Jesus hung on the cross hundreds of years later. The people laughed and scorned Him. They said that if He truly were the Son of God, then God would deliver Him from crucifixion. They didn't realize that Jesus's death was for their sins and was God's plan all along.
- Verse 14: "I am poured out like water, and all my bones are out of joint: my heart is like wax; it is melted in the midst of my bowels." Hanging on the cross would cause the body to experience all these sensations. Jesus's body was stretched severely, which made Him feel as though His bones were out of joint.
- Verse 15: "My strength is dried up like a potsherd; and my tongue cleaveth to my jaws; and thou hast brought me into the dust of death." Hanging on the cross took away all of Jesus's strength. John 19:28 tells us that Jesus said "I thirst" while on the cross.
- Verse 16: "For dogs have compassed me: the assembly of the wicked have enclosed me: they pierced my hands and

my feet." In this passage, dogs represent the people who surrounded the cross, mocking and making fun of Jesus. His hands and feet were pierced as He was nailed to the cross.

- Verse 17: "I may tell all my bones: they look and stare upon me." Jesus could feel all His bones as they were stretched from hanging, as the people were staring at Him on the cross.
- Verse 18: "They part my garments among them, and cast lots upon my vesture." This is exactly what happened: "And they crucified him, and parted his garments, casting lots" (Matthew 27:35). The soldiers cast lots to divide up Jesus's garments.

These verses from Isaiah 53 and Psalm 22 depict exactly what happened to Jesus during His crucifixion. Only through God's divine guidance could Isaiah and the writer of Psalm 22 (probably King David) have foretold all these details hundreds of years before they happened.

None of Jesus's Bones Will Be Broken

Psalm 34:20 foretold this about Jesus: "He keepeth all his bones: not one of them is broken." While Jesus was on the cross, neither of His legs were broken by the soldiers. "Then came the soldiers, and brake the legs of the first, and of the other which was crucified with him. But when they came to Jesus, and saw that he was dead already, they brake not his legs" (John 19:32–33). The soldiers broke the legs of the two men crucified beside Jesus to make sure they would soon die, so their bodies could be taken down before six o'clock that evening as required by Jewish custom. They didn't have to break the legs of Jesus because He was already dead.

People Mourn for Jesus on the Cross

"And they shall look upon me whom they have pierced, and they shall mourn for him, as one mourneth for his only son" (Zechariah 12:10). This prophecy says that Jesus would be pierced and the people would mourn for Him. We read about the fulfillment of this prophecy in John 19:34: "But one of the soldiers with a spear pierced his side, and forthwith came there out blood and water." Jesus's mother and others close to Jesus, including His beloved disciple John, were there to mourn for Him as He hung on the cross for our sins. Jesus looked down and told John to take care of His mother.

Jesus Prophesies Events of His Crucifixion

Probably the most important prophecy about a Messiah was that which Jesus made about Himself. On His final journey to Jerusalem, He foretold to His disciples those things that were going to happen to Him:

> Behold, we go up to Jerusalem; and the Son of man shall be delivered unto the chief priests, and unto the scribes; and they shall condemn him to death, and shall deliver him to the Gentiles. And they shall mock him, and shall scourge him, and shall spit upon him, and shall kill him: and the third day he shall rise again. (Mark 10:33–34)

This passage accurately describes what happened to Jesus leading up to and including His crucifixion and resurrection. He was precise and accurate with each detail.

The list of fulfilled prophecies concerning the coming of the Messiah is long. Every one of them was fulfilled down to the smallest detail through the birth, life, death, and resurrection of Jesus Christ. These fulfilled prophecies suggest that Jesus was indeed the Messiah about whom the prophets spoke in the Old Testament. In the history of all the world, only Jesus satisfied these prophecies.

This chapter completes my brief scan of evidences from several different subject areas that point to a supernatural creator (God) and Jesus Christ as the Messiah. This is only a small sample of what is available. The evidences are there; all you must do is open your eyes to see them.

Part Six

In Summary

Nineteen

Overwhelming Evidence for Christianity

Though this book contains only a small sample of the wealth of evidence supporting the truth and accuracy of the Bible and Christianity, my goal has been to present a compelling argument. If I had included less evidence, one might question the argument presented here, for things do happen by chance. For instance, Micah 5:2 accurately foretells that the Messiah would be born in Bethlehem, but that alone isn't sufficient evidence to claim that Jesus was the Messiah. However, as the evidence increases, the probability of chance and coincidence decreases, as I go on to illustrate below.

The probability of an event happening is a number between 0 and 1, inclusive. An event that cannot possibly happen has a probability of 0, or 0 percent, whereas an event that is certain to occur has a probability of 1, or 100 percent. Each piece of evidence can be assigned a probability based on its strength of support for the Bible and Christianity. Those that provide much support would be assigned higher probabilities than those that provide less support.

In this discussion we will use Bible prophecies of a Messiah that were fulfilled by Jesus to illustrate our case. The assignment of probabilities to the various pieces of evidence is obviously very subjective. Prophecies that foretold of a Messiah and were precisely fulfilled by Jesus centuries later provide strong support for Christianity. For simplicity, lack of better information, and for illustrative purposes only, I will use at least one in one hundred, or 0.01 for Jesus being the Messiah based on each fulfilled prophecy. My intent is to show how the probability of chance and coincidence decreases as the evidence increases.

As discussed in chapter 18, Isaiah 53 describes the events of Christ's crucifixion in exact detail, even though it was written seven to eight hundred years before the birth of Christ. There are only two possibilities—Jesus is the Messiah or Jesus is not the Messiah. Since the probabilities of all possibilities for an event must sum to 1, based on the fulfillment of this one prophecy alone, the probability that Jesus is not the Messiah is no more than $1 - 0.01$, which is 0.99, or 99 percent.

Psalm 22 also prophesied in great detail the events of Christ's crucifixion. Since no prophecy about a Messiah depends on any other prophecy, they are each considered independent events. The probability of multiple independent events is determined by multiplying the probabilities of each of the individual events. Therefore, the probability of Jesus not being the Messiah based only on the two fulfilled prophecies mentioned above would be no more than the result of 0.99 multiplied by 0.99, which is about 0.98, or 98 percent. As this calculation illustrates, as we increase the evidence, the probability of Christianity not being true decreases. Even though some may question the assignment of one in one hundred for the probabilities, regardless of the probabilities we choose for each fulfilled prophecy, the result will always decrease when considering multiple prophecies.

There are differing opinions about the number of Messianic prophecies in the Old Testament that were fulfilled by Jesus, ranging from about two hundred to more than three hundred. To be on the conservative side, let's use the lower figure of two hundred. If we extend our mathematics above, we multiply 0.99 by itself 199 times for a result of about 0.134, or 13.4 percent. These calculations show that for only two hundred fulfilled prophecies the probability of Jesus not being the Messiah dropped significantly.

Even though I used fulfilled prophecies in the calculations above, I could have used any type of evidence for Christianity and assigned probabilities to them. Regardless of the probability we assign to each evidence, if the same logic of mathematical probability is applied to the literally thousands of pieces of evidence, the probability of Christianity not being true would be so small that it would be considered, for all practical purposes, nonexistent. Therefore we should logically conclude that Christianity is the true religion.

Twenty

Beyond the Factual Evidence

The main thrust of this book is to provide evidences for Christianity from various disciplines. However, after presenting and discussing all the various evidences, I want to say this. As a skeptic, I thought it was imperative for me to study and find evidences for the God of the Bible through various disciplines such as archeology, biology, astronomy, and history. But after I really delved into the Bible and obtained a better understanding of it, I found that it presented God's plan so completely and intricately that it had to be the true, inspired Word of God. The Bible was really all I needed after all. The more I sought God, the more He was willing to make Himself available to me.

Beyond accepting evidence for His existence, our God longs for a relationship with us much the same as a father longs for a relationship with his children. He wants to walk with us daily and for us to trust in Him and allow Him into all parts of our lives, regardless of what we may have done in the past or what we may be going through. Lifelong faith is a journey of highs and lows, and over time God molds our hearts and minds to desire what He desires, to love like He loves, and to want to serve Him. All we have to do is invite Him in and trust Him enough to turn things over to Him.

In addition to all the evidences presented in the previous chapters, here are a few other topics that I would like to address. I don't pretend to be a preacher; just want to relay some realizations I've come to.

Personal Growth Through Christianity

If no one ever reads a word of this book, I will still consider the effort to have been a total success. It not only brought me to Christianity, but also revealed to me those things that are what's really important in life. But being a Christian doesn't make us perfect, and I am far from it. We are all sinners by nature and need the grace of God. The only perfect person who ever walked this earth was Jesus Christ.

Over the years, I have done and said things that I truly regret. I was stubborn, had a bad temper, and on many occasions was not tolerant of others. I have disappointed people, but most of all I regret disappointing God. I wish I could go back and undo some of the things that I have said and done. I'm sure there are other people who feel the same way, but we cannot change the past. All we can do is go forward and try to live better lives.

Life Is Precious: Have No Regrets

As I get older, I realize that we shouldn't take life for granted. Like everything else, life is fleeting—gone before we have time to grasp the true meaning of it. We don't know from one day to the next what may happen. We may be perfectly healthy one day and pushing up daisies the next. James, the half-brother of Jesus, wrote, "For what is your life? It is even a vapour, that appeareth for a little time, and then vanisheth away" (James 4:14).

Life is more precious to me with every day that goes by. I see my family, friends, and even pets I love pass from this life, and I cannot imagine never seeing them again. How sad it would be to think that our lives here on earth are all there is for us. There must be more than this, for I don't believe that God would give us our families and friends to love for only the short time we have on earth. What a sad and hopeless situation that would be, if we thought we would never see our loved ones again.

Jesus tells us in the Bible that there is indeed more than the here and now. In John 3:16, He says, "For God so loved the world, that he gave His only begotten Son, that whosoever believeth in him should not perish, but have everlasting life." The Son Jesus speaks of is Himself. The only thing we're required to do to attain everlasting life is to believe that Jesus is the Son of God and accept Him as our Lord and Savior.

Many times I have regretted leaving things unsaid and undone. Often we don't realize such things until it is too late. I wish I could put my arms around every one of my departed Christian family members and friends and tell them how much I love them. But one day I will be able to do just that. This fact gives me great hope and comfort. My life would be filled with much emptiness if I didn't have this realization.

Forgive Others

We should be more tolerant of others, even though we might not agree with them. It may seem difficult at times, but we should be more willing to forgive those things that we feel were done wrongly unto us. Even when it's impossible to forget, we still can forgive. How can we expect God to forgive our sins if we are unwilling to forgive others?

This doesn't mean that we should just lie down and be run over, willingly subjecting ourselves to abuse by others. It is our right and duty to stand up for what is right. That includes all aspects of our lives such as physical, mental, legal, spiritual, and political. I think God expects that of us. God even told the Israelites to go to war with certain nations that opposed them. However, we should always defend ourselves with a humble Christian attitude. It took many years for me to learn that a humble heart will get me much further with people. A hard, unforgiving heart will usually just drive a wedge between me and the other person.

Spiritual World

There is truly a spiritual world in a realm that we cannot see. There is a real heaven and a real hell, as well as angels and demons, and each are referred to throughout the Bible. Angels are mentioned many times in the Bible. For instance, Luke 1:26-38 tells of the angel Gabriel appearing to Mary telling her that she would be the mother of Jesus. Angels appeared to the shepherds in the fields informing them of the birth of Jesus as described in Luke 2:8-20. Acts 12:6-10 documents the angel of the Lord freeing Peter after he was jailed by King Herod. There are many others.

Satan exists, along with his demons, and Jesus mentions these evil beings several times in the Gospels. Jesus even exorcized demons from people who were possessed by them. If you believe in what Jesus said, then you must believe in angels as well as Satan and his demons.

Obviously there are many evil people in this world. Just pick up a newspaper, listen to the news, or just drive down the street and you'll see this evil. I believe that Satan is behind much of the evil in our world. Would you rather be surrounded by evil people or good people? Well, your final destination will determine the group with which you will spend all of eternity.

End-Times Events

When Jesus comes back during the rapture, He will take all believers to be with Him forever. The Bible says that believers will receive their rewards at that time. This leads me to believe that there are varying degrees of rewards for believers, and that our status in heaven will be determined by how we live here on earth. The Bible speaks of those who will be least and those who will be greatest in heaven.

There will be a time of tribulation on earth like the world has never known. I believe this will immediately follow the rapture. During this time, the Antichrist, under the power and guidance of Satan, will rule the entire world. This tribulation will last seven years, as described in the book of Revelation, and it will be considered as a literal hell on earth. I believe that God's purpose for this tribulation will be one last attempt to bring unsaved people to Christ. At the end of the tribulation, Jesus Christ will return in all His glory with His angels, defeat the Antichrist, and establish His millennial kingdom here on earth.

Following Christ's return, there will be the Great White Throne Judgment for the unbelievers as foretold in the book of Revelation. However, if all unbelievers suffer the same judgment, then what would be the purpose? I believe, based on this impending judgment, that there are varying degrees of punishment in the final hell (also called a lake of fire in Revelation) depending upon our actions here on earth. But even the lowest degree of punishment is pure hell, for we would have to spend all eternity apart from God and forever be in the presence of demons, as well as people who were criminals, murderers, and so on while on earth.

Christians May Experience Difficult Times

Christians shouldn't expect everything in their lives to be rosy and problem-free. Satan and his demons target Christians, and he will do all that he can to wreak havoc in their lives. The Old Testament book of Job documents how Satan wanted Job's life destroyed. Satan knows the Bible. He is well aware of his ultimate destiny in hell, and he will try to take as many people as possible with him. Don't be deterred by any hard times you may experience, for if you are a Christian, you will ultimately be rewarded beyond belief. Also, I think God allows certain things to happen so that we will depend on Him more, and our faith may deepen.

Church Is for Everyone

I suspect many poor people do not attend church because they fear being looked down on. They often cannot give much money to the church, and they're intimidated by the big beautiful church buildings and the affluent people who attend. That's sad, because God loves us all regardless of our financial situation.

Just think about the humble life that Jesus lived while here on earth. The King of Kings and Lord of Lords was born in a stable and placed in a manger, a feeding trough for cows. He was raised in a humble family, and his father was a carpenter. After Jesus began His ministry, He told a certain man in Luke 9:58, "Foxes have holes, and birds of the air have nests; but the Son of man hath not where to lay his head." Even though Jesus could have had anything He wanted, I think God planned Jesus's life on earth as an example to show us that our financial or social status doesn't matter, for we are all precious to Him.

Some people feel they have lived a lifestyle that makes them unworthy of being in church, even though they may want to attend. Maybe they've never attended church, but they need to understand that no matter what they have or haven't done, God loves them and is always there for them—if they will just reach out to Him. Even some of the great Bible patriarchs did things that were wrong in God's eyes. King David had an affair with Bathsheba that resulted in a child. Paul, the writer of several New Testament books, persecuted Christians before his conversion to Christianity. God forgave these people, and He will likewise forgive others if only they will ask for it.

Be Christian Witnesses

Jesus told His disciples right before He ascended into heaven, "Go ye into all the world, and preach the gospel to every creature. He that believeth and is baptized shall be saved; but he that believeth not shall be damned" (Mark 16:15–16). Christians cannot all be preachers or Sunday school teachers, but we can reach out to people and tell them about Jesus and His plan of salvation. The most powerful thing we can do is to serve as good Christian examples for other people, for they see our actions as being representative of our true selves. I am certainly speaking to myself here as well.

Christians often find that discussing faith with family members and friends can be more challenging than with strangers, perhaps because we don't want to create tension and animosity between us and those we love. We don't want them to think that we're being self-righteous, judgmental, or simply being nosy. But I think, more importantly, because we realize that close family and friends are familiar with our past actions, we may feel a sense of unworthiness—as we all have fallen short—to enter a discussion on Christianity. As a result, we simply refrain from discussing the subject, which is a real shame.

God and all the angels in heaven rejoice when someone becomes a Christian. God loves every single one of us. After all, He gave his Son Jesus's life for our sins. He let Jesus die a truly agonizing, gruesome death on that cross for us. My, how that must have hurt God! Those of you who have children understand how much God must have loved us to be willing to sacrifice His only Son's life for us so that we might be saved. There is no greater love than that.

Our Souls Are Eternal

We all will die physically someday, but our souls will live for eternity. The question is where our souls will reside for all eternity. If we are Christian, no one should fret, because our souls will be in an eternal place that is great beyond belief, along with the Lord and all the other people who have been saved. We will be reunited for all eternity with our Christian family members and friends who have gone on to be with the Lord. We will all have new bodies and enjoy the happiest times for all eternity.

If we are not Christians, however, we will be in hell with Satan, his demons, and all the other people who were never saved. We will be there in agony for all eternity, for there is no escape. Just think how bad it would be to be locked up in a prison that incarcerates all the worst criminals for the rest of your life on earth, with absolutely no hope for ever getting out. Well, the worst criminals are mild compared with demons. Think about it: no escape from hell for all eternity? How horrifying that would be. Why would anyone take that chance?

Twenty-One

Concluding Remarks

With the vast amount of documented evidence for the Bible, it takes much greater faith to be an atheist than to be a Christian. The Bible explains all aspects of how the world came into existence and God's plan for our redemption. The Bible is the only book that foretells what will happen and how it will all come to pass. The Bible is also the only religious book whose content can be verified through various disciplines.

After reading all the evidence presented here, can you still ignore the possibility of Jesus Christ as depicted in the Bible? After you have died, it will be too late to do anything about where you will spend eternity. If the Bible is true and you're a Christian, you have an eternity that is beautiful and wonderful beyond description to look forward to, along with all your Christian family members and friends who have gone on. If you are not a Christian, however, you will spend eternity in hell. Ultimately we will all end up in one place or the other.

Maybe you think that if there is a heaven, then your goodness and all your good works will get you there. The problem is that no one is good enough by their own actions to enter the kingdom of God. By our nature, we are all sinners, every single one of us. We all have a need for grace. Jesus tells us, "I am the way, the truth, and the life: no man cometh unto the Father, but by me" (John 14:6).

When you have taken your last breath here on earth, the only way to enter heaven is by being a Christian believer, and your profession of Christianity must be genuine, not just lip service. We must believe in and trust the Lord as our savior like little children. Little children usually don't question, and they believe what you tell them. Jesus says, "Verily I say unto you, Except ye be converted, and become like little children, ye shall not enter into the Kingdom of heaven" (Matthew 18:3).

Maybe you have decided that the Bible is the true Word of God, and you want to accept Jesus Christ as your personal Lord and Savior. If so, just get down on your knees and pray to God. Admit that you're a sinner and ask Him for forgiveness of your sins. Tell Him that you accept and trust in Jesus Christ as your Lord and Savior. That's all it takes. You then will have purchased your ticket to heaven for all eternity.

However, if you cannot make this profession in good conscience, I suggest that you begin studying the Bible scriptures and see what they are all about. What do you have to lose? Jesus is knocking at the door. All you have to do is let Him come in. May God truly bless you in your walk with Him or in your search for Him, whichever the case may be.

Notes

Chapter Two: Determine Our Religious Belief/Unbelief

1   Erwin Lutzer, "Keep Eternity in Mind," sermon preached at The Moody Church, Chicago, IL, May 15, 2016, available at *Moody Church Media*, https://www.moodymedia.org/sermons/leaving-legacy/keep-eternity-mind/. Used by Permission.

Chapter Four: A Creator Is Required

1   R. C. Sproul, "Nothing Left to Chance," transcript and video available at "Out of Nothing, Nothing Comes," Nathan W. Bingham, Ligonier Ministries, accessed August 6, 2018, https://www.ligonier.org/blog/out-nothing-nothing-comes/. Used by Permission.

2   Javier Ordovas, "25 Famous Scientists on God," *Aleteia* (June 26, 2014), accessed May 23, 2018, https://aleteia.org/2014/06/26/25-famous-scientists-on-god/. Used by Permission.

3   Hugh Ross, *The Creator and the Cosmos: How the Latest Scientific Discoveries Reveal God* (Colorado Springs, CO: NavPress, 1993), Copyright reverted to Reasons to Believe (RTB), 142. Used by Permission.

4   Ibid.

5   Danny R. Faulkner, "Does the Second Law of Thermodynamics Favor Evolution?" Answers in Genesis (November 3, 2015), accessed November 20, 2017, https://answersingenesis.org/physics/second-law-of-thermodynamics/. Used by Permission.

6   M. Houdmann, P. Matthews-Rose, R. Niles, eds., "Second Law of Thermodynamics," All About Science, Published by AllAboutGod.

com Ministries, 2002-2014, accessed January 9, 2018, https://www.
allaboutscience.org/second-law-of-thermodynamics.htm. Used by
Permission.

7   Hugh Ross, *The Fingerprint of God: Recent Scientific Discoveries
Reveal the Unmistakable Identity of the Creator*, 2nd ed. (Orange, CA:
Promise, 1991), 49. Used by Permission.

8   Ibid, 93.

9   "Six Evidences of a Young Earth," Answers in Genesis, accessed
December 31, 2017, https://answersingenesis.org/evidence-for-creation/
six-evidences-of-young-earth/. Used by Permission.

Chapter Five: Scrapping the Theory of Evolution

1   Charles Darwin, On the Origin of Species (New York: D. Appleton,
1861), chapter 4, 117*, available at http://darwin-online.org.uk/
converted/pdf/1861_OriginNY_F382.pdf.

2   Ibid., chapter 4, 121*.

3   Henry M. Morris, "Does Entropy Contradict Evolution?" *Acts &
Facts* 14, no. 3 (March 1, 1985), Institute for Creation Research, ICR.
org, accessed May 21, 2018, http://www.icr.org/article/does-entropy-
contradict-evolution/. Used by Permission.

4   Paul S. Taylor, "Second Law of Thermodynamics: Does This Basic
Law of Nature Prevent Evolution?" Christian Answers Network,
accessed November 20, 2017, https://christiananswers.net/q-eden/edn-
thermodynamics.html. Used by Permission.

5   Ibid.

6   RadioTimes, "Secrets of the Brain," Immediate Media, accessed
December 26, 2017, http://www.radiotimes.com/news/2016-01-21/
secrets-of-the-brain/. Used by Permission.

7   Darwin, 154.

8   Darwin, 154.

9   Darwin, 154.

10   Darwin, 154–155.

Chapter Six: A Designer Is Required

1 Hugh Ross, *The Creator and the Cosmos: How the Latest Scientific Discoveries Reveal God* (Colorado Springs, CO: NavPress, 1993), Copyright reverted to Reasons to Believe (RTB), 128. Used by Permission.
2 Ibid., 129.

Chapter Eight: The Bible: Its Survival and Harmony

1 Mike Matthews, "The Preservation of the Bible," Answers in Genesis, accessed April 28, 2018, https://answersingenesis.org/the-word-of-god/the-preservation-of-the-bible. Used by Permission.
2 Ibid.
3 Ibid.
4 Ibid.

Chapter Ten: Jewish Feasts Point to Jesus as the Messiah

1 Edward Chumney, *The Seven Festivals of the Messiah* (Shippensburg, PA: Treasure House, 1994), 10. Used by Permission.
2 Ibid., 9.
3 Ibid., 24.
4 Ibid., 45–46
5 Ibid., 46.
6 Ibid., 61.
7 Ibid., 62.

Chapter Eleven: Health Instructions from God to the Israelites

1 Kyle Butt, "Scientific Foreknowledge and Medical Acumen of the Bible," (Montgomery, AL: Apologetics Press, 2006), accessed August 8, 2018, https://apologeticspress.org/apcontent.aspx?category=13&article=2024. Used by Permission.
2 Bert Thompson, "Biblical Accuracy and Circumcision on the 8th Day," (Montgomery, AL: Apologetics Press, 1993), accessed December 17, 2017, http://apologeticspress.org/apcontent.aspx?category=13&article=1118. Used by Permission.

Chapter Twelve: Real People, Places, and Events Mentioned in the Bible

1   Randall Price, *The Stones Cry Out: What Archaeology Reveals About the Truth of the Bible* (Eugene, OR: Harvest House, 1997), www. harvesthousepublishers.com, Copyright 1997 by Word of the Bible Ministries, 28. Used by Permission.

2   Ibid., 35.

3   Ibid., 266–267.

4   Amish Shah, "The Ebla Tablets Mystery," originally published at AncientExplorers.com of Deep Origins, accessed July 19, 2018, available at https://projectyourself.com/blogs/news/the-ebla-tablets-mystery. Used by Permission.

5   Ibid.

Chapter Thirteen: Prophecies About People, Places, and Events Mentioned in the Bible

1   J. Varner Wallace, "From Reliable to Divine: Fulfilled Prophecy in the Old Testament," Cold-Case Christianity (April 11, 2018), accessed August 2, 2018, http://coldcasechristianity.com/2018/from-reliable-to-divine-fulfilled-prophecy-in-the-old-testament/. Used by Permission.

2   Randall Price, *The Stones Cry Out: What Archaeology Reveals About the Truth of the Bible* (Eugene, OR: Harvest House, 1997), www. harvesthousepublishers.com, Copyright 1997 by Word of the Bible Ministries, 258. Used by Permission.

3   "Zion Would Be 'Plowed Like a Field,'" AboutBibleProphecy.com, accessed December 12, 2017, http://www.aboutbibleprophecy.com/ micah_3_11.htm. Used by Permission.

Chapter Fourteen: Accurate Prophecies Involving Biblical Time Intervals

1   David R. Reagan, "Daniel's 70 Weeks of Years," Lamb & Lion Ministries, accessed June 13, 2018, http://christinprophecy.org/articles/ daniels-70-weeks-of-years/. Used by Permission.

2   Robert J. Morgan, "Jeremiah's Seventy Years," accessed November 13, 2017, http://www.robertjmorgan.com/uncategorized/jeremiahs-seventy-years/. Used by Permission.

Chapter Sixteen: Historical Documents That Support the Bible

1   William Whiston, trans., *The Complete Works of Flavius Josephus* (1737), Passages taken from *The Antiquities of the Jews*, book 18, chapter 3, accessed July 20, 2018, http://www.ultimatebiblereferencelibrary.com/Complete_Works_of_Josephus.pdf.

2   Ibid., book 18, chapter 5.

3   Ibid., book 18, chapter 5.

4   Ibid., book 6, chapter 8.

5   Ibid., book 6, chapter 8.

Chapter Seventeen: Jesus, His Disciples, and Early Christians

1   Sam Storms, "10 Things You Should Know About the Empty Tomb of Jesus," Sam Storms: Enjoying God, accessed May 24, 2018, http://www.samstorms.com/enjoying-god-blog/post/10-things-you-should-know-about-the-empty-tomb-of-jesus. Used by Permission.

Printed in the United States
by Baker & Taylor Publisher Services